A Practical Guide to Logistic Regression Using Stata

A Practical Guide to Logistic Regression Using Stata

Alan C. Acock
Oregon State University

A Stata Press Publication
StataCorp LLC
College Station, Texas

Published by Stata Press, 4905 Lakeway Drive, College Station, Texas 77845
Typeset in LaTeX 2ε
Printed in the United States of America
10 9 8 7 6 5 4 3 2 1

Print ISBN-10: 1-59718-415-2
Print ISBN-13: 978-1-59718-415-1
ePub ISBN-10: 1-59718-416-0
ePub ISBN-13: 978-1-59718-416-8

Library of Congress Control Number: 2026934499

Contents

List of figures ix

List of tables xi

List of boxes xiii

Preface xv

Acknowledgments xvii

1 What we can do with logistic regression 1

1.1 Questions we can answer using logistic regression . . . 1

1.2 Ways to report results . . . 2

1.3 Using Stata . . . 4

2 Getting ready 7

2.1 Opening the dataset . . . 7

2.2 Exploring the data . . . 8

2.3 Labeling values for categorical variables . . . 10

2.4 Saving the edited dataset . . . 13

3 Conventional ordinary least-squares regression versus logistic regression 15

3.1 What OLS regression can tell us . . . 15

3.2 What logistic regression can tell us . . . 20

3.2.1 Robust and cluster–robust estimation . . . 24

An imperfect model . . . 25

Clustered sample design . . . 26

4 Interpreting an odds ratio 29

4.1 What is an odds ratio? . . . 29

4.2 Interpreting ORs as a percentage difference for binary predictors . . . 31

5 **What is wrong with ordinary least-squares regression for a binary outcome?** **35**

5.1 Hypothetical data 35

5.2 How does logistic regression fit better than ordinary least-squares linear regression? 37

6 **Fitting and interpreting logistic regression models** **39**

6.1 Interpreting coefficients and odds ratios 39

6.2 Fitting logistic regression models with multiple predictors 41

6.3 Interpreting ORs for quantitative predictors 42

6.4 Selecting the right base level for categorical predictors 44

7 **How well does the model fit the data?** **47**

7.1 Pseudo-R^2 measures of fit 47

7.2 Information criteria 52

7.3 Identifying cases that the model fits poorly 53

8 **Sensitivity and specificity** **55**

8.1 Criteria for evaluating an analysis 55

8.2 Estimation of sensitivity and specificity 57

9 **Receiver operating characteristic curves and cutpoints for screening tests** **59**

9.1 ROC curves 60

9.2 Comparing tests 66

10 **Predictions using the margins command** **69**

10.1 What is better than reporting coefficients and odds ratios? 69

10.2 Data preparation 69

10.3 Estimating the ORs 71

10.4 The margins command 72

10.4.1 Estimating risk for categorical predictors 72

10.4.2 Estimating the risk for quantitative predictors 74

10.4.3 Estimating for a combination of categorical and quantitative variables 75

11 Graphic presentation using the marginsplot command 79

11.1 When and why . . . 79

11.2 Graphs of categorical predictors that include three or more categories 79

11.3 Graphs with one quantitative predictor . . . 86

11.4 Graphs with one quantitative and one categorical predictor . . . 89

11.5 Graphs of a pair of categorical predictors . . . 90

11.6 Graphs with a pair of quantitative predictors . . . 91

12 Curve fitting with quadratic models 93

12.1 A hypothetical example of a quadratic model using OLS regression . 93

12.2 Estimating the curve (uncentered predictor) . . . 97

12.3 Centering, collinearity, and nonessential collinearity . . . 102

12.4 Estimating the curve (centered x) . . . 103

12.5 Compare centered and uncentered models . . . 105

12.6 Use of a quadratic with logistic regression . . . 106

13 Interaction 115

13.1 Introduction . . . 115

13.2 Interaction of a categorical and a quantitative variable using logistic regression . . . 117

13.3 Estimating and interpreting probabilities (uncentered) . . . 119

13.4 Interaction of categorical variables . . . 124

13.5 Interaction of quantitative variables . . . 127

14 Running nestreg and postestimation commands 133

14.1 Nested logistic regression . . . 134

14.2 Selected postestimation commands . . . 138

15 Special topics 145

15.1 Collinearity and multicollinearity . . . 145

15.1.1 Evaluating multicollinearity . . . 146

15.2 Sample size . . . 148

15.3 Small-sample bias . . . 151

15.4 Relative risk . . . 153

A Appendix **159**

References **167**

Author index **171**

Subject index **173**

Figures

1.1 Risk of high blood pressure by BMI 4

3.1 Distribution of residuals from model predicting birthweight 20

5.1 Scatterplot comparing linear and logistic regressions with raw data . 37

9.1 ROC curve 64
9.2 ROC curves comparing math test with science test 67

11.1 High blood pressure and self-reported health 82
11.2 High blood pressure and self-reported health (edited) 86
11.3 BMI and high blood pressure 88
11.4 Effect of gender and BMI on high blood pressure 89
11.5 Effects of gender and self-reported health on high blood pressure . . 90
11.6 Effects of age with BMI on high blood pressure 91

12.1 Length of sessions and test scores 95
12.2 Length of sessions and test scores using a lowess curve 96
12.3 A linear regression provides a terrible and misleading fit to the data 97
12.4 A curve showing the effect of a session length (uncentered) 101
12.5 A curve showing the effect of centered session length on the score . . 105
12.6 Estimated logit of high blood pressure predicted by BMI 107
12.7 Estimated probability (additive model without quadratic term) . . . 109
12.8 Estimated probability (quadratic model—uncentered) 112
12.9 Estimated probability (quadratic model—centered) 114

13.1 Interaction of gender and age predicting high blood pressure (uncentered) 121
13.2 The large advantage of women decreases with age (uncentered) . . . 123
13.3 Interaction of gender and health predicting risk of high blood pressure 125
13.4 Women's advantage for those reporting good or better health 127
13.5 Age and BMI predicting risk without interaction 129
13.6 Age and BMI predicting with interaction 132

Tables

6.1 Regression Bs and corresponding ORs 40

7.1 Guide to comparing the fits of two models 52

8.1 Sensitivity and specificity 55

Boxes

2.1 What about binary variables coded as 1 and 2? 10

2.2 The working directory 14

3.1 Stata's `logistic` and `logit` commands 22

5.1 How is logistic regression a linear model? 38

6.1 How does Stata know that you have reached the end of a command? 42

Preface

Logistic regression is widely used throughout many scientific disciplines. Your reading of this preface indicates that you are in one of these disciplines. Logistic regression is the prime choice for any research that classifies observations into binary groups, such as success versus failure. To illustrate how widely logistic regression is used, Alan Rowberg suggested that I ask PubMed, so I searched for the term "logistic regression", which produced a list of 52,082 publications at the time of this writing. Although logistic regression is widely used, its results often are misinterpreted or fail to provide the best possible interpretation. In this book, I aim to present the best ways to interpret logistic regression for both professional and lay audiences.

Suppose that you read an article in a medical journal and find a statement that a mother being a smoker significantly increases the likelihood of her newborn having a low birthweight because the coefficient is positive and the p-value is small. The article might list a coefficient and an odds ratio in a table without much interpretation. You should be careful with statements like this. The p-value may be small even when the effect has no practical significance, so it is important to ask questions that may help your interpretation of the results. What is the strength of the impact? What additional risk or reduction in risk does smoking contribute? What graphs would help readers visualize the relationship?

In this book, I will report the p-value of findings, but my focus is on practical significance rather than statistical significance. A small p-value does not mean that the effect has any practical importance, especially with large samples. Because of this, I am following the suggestion of Wasserstein and Lazar (2016) and not using a specific cutoff, such as $p < 0.05$, as evidence of significance.

Do you have enough statistical background to use this book? Yes, if you have

1. completed a single introductory course in statistics and
2. have a basic knowledge of Stata.

Even if you have a more advanced background, this book can still teach you Stata tricks and the best use of logistic regression.

How to use this book. The chapters in this book are short and focus on specific applications of logistic regression. Ideally, you will work through this short book from beginning to end. However, you may wish to refer back to individual chapters as needed, so there is some duplication of content to allow chapters to stand alone. The appendix includes a do-file that reproduces nearly everything covered in this book. This do-file should be a valuable reference to consult for your research.

Acknowledgments

A key advantage of Stata Press is its comprehensive support for a book of this type. Other publishers would not have the level of support and expertise I received from Stata Press.

I owe a huge debt to Chuck Huber, Stata's Director of Statistical Outreach. He reviewed a few very early chapters. In addition to providing content suggestions, Chuck was a great motivator. Without his encouragement, this book would never have been completed.

My draft of the book was assigned to Kristin MacDonald, Stata's Executive Director for Statistical Services. She went over every word in multiple revisions to make the book as technically strong as it is. The book benefited from her finding optimal ways to conduct analysis using Stata commands. Kristin's contributions are a great advantage for the reader because she provided many suggestions that make the book more direct, easier to understand, and more efficient.

I also want to thank Adam Crawley, who was the English editor for this book. Finally, Stephanie White, Stata's Senior Production Associate, put this book together.

1 What we can do with logistic regression

1.1 Questions we can answer using logistic regression

Logistic regression is appropriate when we wish to model whether something happens. For example, we can learn what factors predict the following:

- Who is more likely to become a type 2 diabetic?
- Who preorders an experimental electric bike on a GoFundMe campaign?
- Which newborns will have a low birthweight?
- What children are ready for the first grade?
- Who drops out of college?
- Who is most likely to vote?
- Which newlyweds will get divorced in the first five years of their marriage?

Not all applications start with a dichotomy like those above. For example, does a mother being a smoker raise the risk of a low birthweight for her newborn? Though birthweight is a quantitative variable, we would generate a binary variable, an indicator of low birthweight, to answer this question by using logistic regression.

Because the World Health Organization defines low birthweight as less than 2,500 grams, our new variable would have categories for a birthweight of less than 2,500 grams and for a birthweight of 2,500 grams or more. The difference between 2,475 grams and 2,525 grams is less than 2 ounces, but one weight is in the category of all birthweights less than 2,500 grams, while the other weight is in the category of birthweights from 2,500 grams to the heaviest child ever born.

A second example is predicting who will graduate from college. Suppose that one's education is coded as 1 for "Less than high school", 2 for "High school", 3 for "Some college", 4 for "College graduate", and 5 for "Postgraduate". We create a new binary variable by combining codes 1–3 to indicate those who have not graduated college and combining codes 4–5 to indicate those who have. This variable lets us answer our question but ignores the difference between "Less than high school" and "Some college".

Information is lost when we dichotomize a quantitative variable, so we should do so only when the dichotomy is the focus of our research question.

1.2 Ways to report results

Once we have determined that logistic regression is appropriate for our research question, we perform the analysis and report the results. Logistic regression results typically report which independent variables are statistically significant and the directions of their effects. Often, this is insufficient. How can we present logistic regression results that are meaningful to both professional and lay audiences?

Let us explore alternative ways of presenting results by using an example of logistic regression that models the relationship between obesity and the risk (probability) of high blood pressure. There are many measures of obesity. One of them is body mass index (BMI), which is based on a person's height and weight. It is defined as

$$\text{BMI} = \frac{\text{Weight(kg)}}{\text{Height(m)}^2}$$

Alternatively, it is defined using imperial measures as

$$\text{BMI} = \frac{\text{Weight(lb)} \times 703}{\text{Height(in)}^2}$$

BMI ignores body composition and is a crude measure of obesity. Nonetheless, it is widely used because it requires knowing only a person's weight and height.

Consider Dr. Ahmed Jones's advice to his patient of 15 years, Monica. For each visit, Dr. Jones's nurse checks Monica's weight and height. From these results, the nurse records Monica's BMI. Dr. Jones notes that Monica's BMI has drifted higher. Over the last 15 years, her BMI of 22 has increased to 32. According to standard BMI guidelines, a BMI of 22 is healthy, but 32 is obese.

Because clinically high blood pressure is a binary outcome (you either have it or do not have it), logistic regression is an appropriate statistical tool to model it. Based on the results of a logistic regression, Dr. Jones could tell Monica that obesity has a statistically significant effect on the risk of high blood pressure, but this may not convince Monica to modify her diet and exercise program. What is better than reporting just the statistical significance or p-values? Because a statistically significant effect does not equal a practically substantial effect, Dr. Jones should explain the practical significance. If he does not do this, it will be easy for Monica to dismiss his advice. What evidence might convince Monica of the danger of a high BMI?

Let us assume that Dr. Jones recently read in a medical article that the logistic regression coefficient (B) of BMI predicting high blood pressure is 0.149, $p < 0.001$. This B is the difference in the natural logarithm of the odds of high blood pressure for a one-point difference in BMI. The interpretation of this is not transparent even to an academic audience, so it is even less helpful to a typical patient; most people have yet to learn what $B = 0.149$, $p < 0.001$ would mean. Additionally, Monica needs to understand the estimated risk that she will have high blood pressure now that her BMI has increased by 10 points.

Dr. Jones might exponentiate the B, that is, determine e^B, and tell Monica that the odds ratio (OR) is 1.16. The OR is easier to understand than the B. However, this approach has three potential problems:

1. Monica may not understand how to interpret an OR of 1.16.
2. The OR is for a one-point difference in Monica's BMI, for example, from 22 to 23, not for her 10-point difference from 22 to 32. It is not as simple as saying that the odds for a 10-point difference would be 1.16 times 10 as great.
3. The OR is not an estimate of the difference in the risk of high blood pressure associated with BMIs of 22 versus 32. The effect of her BMI on her risk of having high blood pressure is easier to understand than the OR. Neither the B nor the OR is a direct measure of what has happened to Monica's risk of high blood pressure.

Monica needs to learn her risk of high blood pressure at a BMI of 32 compared with her risk at a BMI of 22. To illustrate this for Monica, Dr. Jones could estimate her risk of having high blood pressure ($\text{Pr} = 0.300$) with a BMI of 22 compared with the risk ($\text{Pr} = 0.654$) with a BMI of 32.

Dr. Jones might express these values as percentages. He estimates that Monica's risk of high blood pressure is 30.0% with a BMI of 22, but it is 65.4% with a BMI of 32. Her increased BMI more than doubles her risk of high blood pressure.

If the article reported the estimated risk by BMI level and the relationship had included a graph, Dr. Jones could show it (see figure 1.1) to Monica. Unfortunately, many researchers stop after reporting the B or OR and whether they are statistically significant. Figure 1.1 allows Monica to see more than the effects of her past and current BMI. It shows that by losing weight and reducing her BMI, she could dramatically lower her risk of high blood pressure.

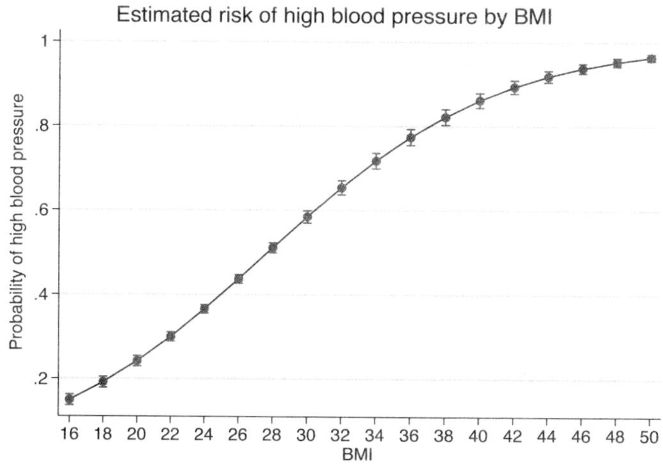

Figure 1.1. Risk of high blood pressure by BMI

1.3 Using Stata

Stata makes it easy to perform logistic regression and obtain the results you want to report. Throughout this book, I will demonstrate how to use Stata for each analysis. If you use another software package such as SAS, R, or SPSS, you can still use this book to learn what you should report to make sense of logistic regression. Many Stata commands have parallel commands in other statistical packages. However, note that even if your data are stored in the format of another package such as SPSS or SAS, you can analyze these data using Stata. It is easy to import SPSS and SAS datasets into a Stata dataset. This will allow you to take full advantage of this book even if you primarily use SPSS or SAS. To do so using Stata's menu system, click on **File > Import > SPSS data (*.sav)** to import an SPSS dataset. Click on **File > Import > SAS XPORT Version 8 (*.v8xpt)** to open a SAS export file. Alternatively, you can click on **File > Import > SAS data (*.sas7bdat)** to import a SAS dataset.

Stata's menu system and dialog boxes make it easy to learn. Alternatively, you can use Stata's parsimonious and consistent commands. These commands can be entered directly into the Command window or into a do-file (see appendix). Each command begins with the command's name followed by a list of variables. With regression commands, the outcome variable is the first variable in the variable list.

Following Stata convention, a dot and a blank space (.) are placed in front of Stata commands when they appear on a separate line in the text. The dot and space are there to draw your attention to the command, but the result is the same whether or not we enter the dot and space. When I mention a Stata command or variable name, I will put it in typewriter font. I will also use typewriter font when naming datasets and when referring to elements of a dataset or output.

Here is an example of how this looks for a logistic regression command to predict whether a newborn will have a low birthweight. It will produce the ORs for the effect of the mother's age and whether she smoked during pregnancy:

```
. logistic low age smoke
```

This command runs logistic regression to predict the outcome variable `low`. A mother's age and whether she was a smoker are the independent variables. At the end of the command, we could add options as available to modify the command.

Stata has a maxim, "type a little, get a little", in how commands are designed. As a result, we sometimes use postestimation commands, which use the results of the initial command to provide further analysis. Stata's postestimation commands for logistic regression provide extended results that help us interpret the standard results.

All Stata commands use lowercase type. I recommend using lowercase for variable names as well. Stata is case sensitive, so `age`, `Age`, and `AGE` would be three different variables. SAS and SPSS are not case sensitive, so if you import a dataset from them, you may find that variable names are all capitalized or use both uppercase and lowercase. You can convert variable names to lowercase when importing them. You can also convert variable names to lowercase when you encounter a Stata dataset that capitalizes some or all variable names with the simple Stata command `rename`. For example,

```
. rename ID-ZODIAC, lower
```

will convert all variables from `ID` to `ZODIAC` to lowercase. If there are variables that have the same letters, differing only in capitalization, Stata reports how it manages those variables.

Different academic and research areas use different names for the outcome variable we are predicting and the variables used to predict it. Variables that predict an outcome may be called independent variables, covariates, or simply predictors. The outcome variable we predict may be called the dependent, response, or predicted variable. There are conceptual reasons for these name choices in different fields, but I will not discuss them here.

As you work through this book, I urge you to

1. always have Stata open,
2. run each command as you work your way through the book, and
3. save your commands in your do-file.

I have included a do-file in the appendix that runs nearly everything in the book. The appendix can serve as a reference for your work when using Stata in your logistic regression applications.

2 Getting ready

2.1 Opening the dataset

In this chapter, we will use a dataset named lbw.dta (Hosmer, Lemeshow, and Sturdivant 2013), which is used in the *Stata Base Reference Manual*. If you are connected to the internet, you can load the data at any time by typing

```
. webuse lbw
(Hosmer & Lemeshow data)
```

in the Command window. This command will open the dataset in Stata. If another dataset is open, you must first run the clear command. I recommend that you load lbw.dta now so that you can follow along with the examples in this chapter. Many people find working along with examples to be helpful.

lbw.dta includes variables related to a newborn's risk of having a low birthweight. The variable low indicates whether the birthweight is considered to be low (defined as less than 2,500 grams). Newborns with a birthweight below 2,500 grams are coded as 1, and newborns with a birthweight of 2,500 grams or higher are coded as 0. Low birthweight is coded as 1 because it signifies the presence of the condition we are predicting. Note that we are not predicting the actual birthweight measured in grams, bwt, but only whether the newborn's birthweight is low.

Our possible predictors include the age of the mother (age), her weight at her last menstruation (lwt), whether she smoked during pregnancy (smoke), whether she has a history of hypertension (ht), and how often she visited a physician during her first trimester (ftv).

Our focus will be on the effect of smoking during pregnancy on the probability of having a clinically low-birthweight newborn.

Our primary research question is as follows:

> Does a mother who smoked during pregnancy increase the probability of her newborn having a low birthweight, controlling for selected covariates?

2.2 Exploring the data

It is essential to know as much as we can about any data we are going to analyze. How were they collected? Who funded them? How were variables measured? Were the data used in refereed publications? Here we will describe only the variables, how they were measured, and their distributions. We first use Stata's `describe` command:

```
. describe

Contains data from https://www.stata-press.com/data/r19/lbw.dta
 Observations:           189                  Hosmer & Lemeshow data
    Variables:            11                  15 Jan 2024 05:01
--------------------------------------------------------------------------------
Variable      Storage   Display    Value
    name         type    format    label      Variable label
--------------------------------------------------------------------------------
id              int     %8.0g                 Identification code
low             byte    %8.0g                 Birthweight<2500g
age             byte    %8.0g                 Age of mother
lwt             int     %8.0g                 Weight at last menstrual period
race            byte    %8.0g      race       Race
smoke           byte    %9.0g      smoke      Smoked during pregnancy
ptl             byte    %8.0g                 Premature labor history (count)
ht              byte    %8.0g                 Has history of hypertension
ui              byte    %8.0g                 Presence, uterine irritability
ftv             byte    %8.0g                 Number of visits to physician
                                                during 1st trimester
bwt             int     %8.0g                 Birthweight (grams)
--------------------------------------------------------------------------------
Sorted by:
```

If we just wanted to describe a subset of variables, we would run the `describe` command followed by a list of those variables. `describe` gives us

1. the variable names,
2. the storage types,
3. which categorical variables have value labels (`race` and `smoke` do, but `low` and `ht` do not), and
4. the variable labels.

Next run the **summarize** command in the Command window. We will summarize the variables we use in this chapter:

```
. summarize age lwt bwt smoke ht race low ftv

    Variable |        Obs        Mean    Std. dev.       Min        Max
-------------+---------------------------------------------------------
         age |        189     23.2381    5.298678         14         45
         lwt |        189    129.8201    30.57515         80        250
         bwt |        189    2944.286     729.016        709       4990
       smoke |        189    .3915344    .4893898          0          1
          ht |        189    .0634921    .2444936          0          1
-------------+---------------------------------------------------------
        race |        189    1.846561    .9183422          1          3
         low |        189    .3121693    .4646093          0          1
         ftv |        189    .7936508    1.059286          0          6
```

We have 189 observations for every variable. This is a small sample for logistic regression (see section 15.2). Two of our potential predictors are binary variables: whether the mother was a smoker (smoke) and whether she had hypertension (ht). Both were coded as 0 if she did not or 1 if she did. The race variable has three nominal categories, coded as 1–3, and the number of visits to a physician during the first trimester (ftv) has seven categories, coded as 0–6. Depending on the specific analysis, the ftv variable might be treated as quantitative or an ordered categorical variable with seven categories. Two predictor variables are quantitative—the mother's age (age) and her weight at the last menstrual period (lwt). We assume that age and lwt are quantitative because of the range of values in the columns labeled Min and Max.

Notice that the hypertension binary variable, ht, has a mean of just 0.063. Because ht is coded as 0 or 1, only 6.3% of the study participants were classified as hypertensive, that is, were coded as 1. This interpretation would not be available if the variables were coded as 1 or 2. With a small sample ($N = 189$), we have only 12 mothers who reported having hypertension. This may give us little power to generalize the effect of hypertension to a larger population.

There is a similar problem with the frequency of doctor visits. The mean for ftv is 0.794, but ftv ranges from 0 to 6. This means that few mothers had more than one or two visits. The ftv variable has a strong positive skew. We might want to dichotomize ftv to see whether the mothers had any visits.

Many datasets use codes of 1 and 2 for binary variables, with 1 for "No" and 2 for "Yes". I recommend recoding any such variable to instead use codes of 0 and 1. Stata requires this for outcome variables in logistic regression (see box 2.1). In logistic regression, Stata fits a model for the probability that the outcome is 1 (or more specifically, the probability that the outcome is not 0). Often, an outcome of 1 corresponds to a positive result. In our example of low birthweight, we are predicting a negative outcome. Some publications are not clear enough about which outcome is coded as 1. Being explicit about your coding in your writing can avoid gross misinterpretations.

Box 2.1. What about binary variables coded as 1 and 2?

Many datasets use values of 1 and 2 for recording binary variables. If your data do this, I recommend recoding the variables to 0 and 1, where 0 signifies the absence of the condition, or "no" and 1 signifies the presence of the condition, or "yes". I recommend doing this recoding for all your binary variables, but it is necessary only for outcome variables. Using codes of 0 and 1 for binary variables is often referred to as "dummy variable" coding.

What happens if you mistakenly leave the outcome variable with codes of 1 and 2? When you run logistic regression, you get the following error message:

```
outcome does not vary; remember:
                                  0 = negative outcome,
         all other nonmissing values = positive outcome
r(2000);
```

This error message indicates that there are 0 negative cases. This is because Stata looks to the code of 0 for a negative case. Codes of 1 or 2 are both treated as positive, so this coding is interpreted as having all positive cases.

2.3 Labeling values for categorical variables

I will cover only a few basic data management procedures[1] that we should know before we fit logistic regression models with the dataset. It is helpful for categorical variables to have clear labels to go with the coded values. The value labels clarify the logistic regression results. Stata has a two-step method of assigning value labels:

1. We use `label define` to create a value label and give it a nickname, for example, `yesno`. The nickname we pick is arbitrary.
2. We use `label values` to apply the label with this nickname to each appropriate variable.

The pair of commands is

```
. label define yesno 0 "No" 1 "Yes"
. label values ht low yesno
```

The first command defines the nickname, `yesno`, so that `No` is the value label for codes of 0 and `Yes` is the value label for codes of 1. The second command assigns these value labels to both binary variables, `ht` and `low`. Any number of variables can use the same assignment and nickname.

1. Mitchell (2020) has an excellent book called *Data Management Using Stata*. His book is wonderfully accessible and will make you a highly qualified data manager!

Let us check on our value labels by rerunning the **describe** command, including all the variables we use in this book:

```
. describe age lwt bwt smoke ht race low ftv

Variable      Storage   Display    Value
    name         type    format    label      Variable label
------------------------------------------------------------------------------
age             byte    %8.0g                 Age of mother
lwt             int     %8.0g                 Weight at last menstrual period
bwt             int     %8.0g                 Birthweight (grams)
smoke           byte    %9.0g      smoke      Smoked during pregnancy
ht              byte    %8.0g      yesno      Has history of hypertension
race            byte    %8.0g      race       Race
low             byte    %8.0g      yesno      Birthweight<2500g
ftv             byte    %8.0g                 Number of visits to physician
                                                during 1st trimester
```

The `yesno` nickname appears under the `Value label` column for `ht` and `low`.

Whenever we change a variable, we should confirm that our change worked as intended. We will do so with the `fre` command. Note that `fre` is a community-contributed command written by Jann (2007). `fre` produces a frequency distribution. It includes both the numerical code and the value label for each code, which is useful because although Stata's `tabulate` command can also be used, it does not report the code and the value label together.

You can download and install the `fre` command on your computer by typing the following in your Command window:[2]

```
. ssc install fre
```

2. Normally, community-contributed commands will be installed on your computer permanently, so `fre` will be available whenever you need it. However, some lab computers have all changes erased each day because of security procedures. If you are using such a system, you may need to reinstall the `fre` command when you need to use it.

After we run `fre`, the frequency distributions appear in the Results window:

```
. fre low ht
low — Birthweight<2500g
```

		Freq.	Percent	Valid	Cum.
Valid	0 No	130	68.78	68.78	68.78
	1 Yes	59	31.22	31.22	100.00
	Total	189	100.00	100.00	

```
ht — Has history of hypertension
```

		Freq.	Percent	Valid	Cum.
Valid	0 No	177	93.65	93.65	93.65
	1 Yes	12	6.35	6.35	100.00
	Total	189	100.00	100.00	

The value labels functioned as intended, but the `fre` command revealed one issue. We sensed this issue earlier, given the low mean of 0.063 for the `ht` variable: only 12 of our 189 mothers reported a history of hypertension. From a strictly statistical perspective, the distribution of an independent variable poses no problem for estimating regression parameters. However, because the dataset contains only 12 women who had hypertension, there may not be enough data to obtain a reliable estimate of the effect of hypertension.

The variable `race` already has a value label with the same nickname as `race`. This variable has three categories: 1 for `White`, 2 for `Black`, and 3 for `Other`.

```
. fre race
race — Race
```

		Freq.	Percent	Valid	Cum.
Valid	1 White	96	50.79	50.79	50.79
	2 Black	26	13.76	13.76	64.55
	3 Other	67	35.45	35.45	100.00
	Total	189	100.00	100.00	

The `Other` category is problematic because it lumps multiple races and ethnicities together, for example, Latinx, Asian, Indigenous Peoples, and mixed races. Mothers of different races in this category may have different risks of having a low-birthweight newborn. Making things more problematic, `Other` is more than one-third of the total sample. We will keep this category to illustrate working with categorical predictors with three or more categories.

2.4 Saving the edited dataset

At this point, we should save the dataset that includes our changes. We will save our revised file as `lbw_working.dta`. By default, it will be saved in the current working directory (see box 2.2). At the bottom of the Stata interface, we will find the default working directory. For Windows, this might say

```
C:\Users\Stata\Documents\Stata
```

For Mac, it might say

```
/Users/Documents/Stata
```

If your Stata interface shows a different working directory, do not worry; you can use that one. To save our revised dataset to our working directory, we type

```
. save "lbw_working", replace
file lbw_working.dta saved
```

Note that we added the `replace` option,[3] which overwrites any existing dataset named `lbw_working.dta`. We also included quotation marks around the filename. These can be omitted but are necessary if the filename includes a space. From now on, to open `lbw_working.dta`, we run

```
. use "lbw_working", clear
(Hosmer & Lemeshow data)
```

We added the `clear` option, which replaces whatever dataset we currently have open. `clear` permanently erases the dataset we had open if we did not save it.

3. Note that the comma comes after the quotation marks.

Box 2.2. The working directory

Your data are stored in your current working directory, whose name appears in the small print at the bottom of the Stata interface. Here is what this looks like on my own Mac:

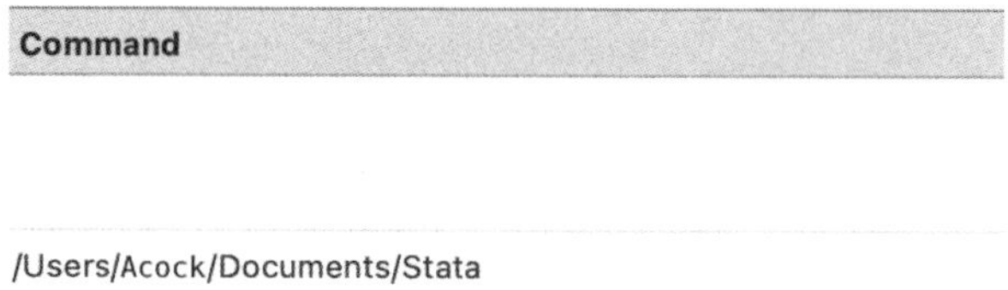

You might want to save a file to a different directory or have each of your projects in its own working directory. If you want to change the working directory, click on **File** > **Change working directory...**. Then click on **New Folder** and enter the name you pick for that project—for example, you might add a folder called `Logistic Regression` and then pick it. If I did this, then in the line below the Command window, I would see `/Users/Acock/Documents/Logistic Regression`.

If you change your working directory, you need to check the current working directory each time you open Stata and change it if needed.

When you open Stata, check the bottom of the screen to ensure that it is using the appropriate working directory. If it is not the right one for your project, you can click on **File** > **Change working directory...** and select the correct one.

3 Conventional ordinary least-squares regression versus logistic regression

This chapter will show the advantages of logistic regression over conventional ordinary least-squares (OLS) regression for a binary outcome variable. Advanced users may want to skip this chapter.

First, we open the working dataset we generated and saved in chapter 2. (If you did not create the working dataset in chapter 2, you can run the commands in the chapter 2 section of the do-file in the appendix.) To open the working dataset using the menu system, we will click on **File** > **Open recent** and select `lbw_working.dta`. If you saved the working file to the current working directory on your computer, you could also open it with this simple command:

```
. use "lbw_working"
(Hosmer & Lemeshow data)
```

If you want to retrieve a dataset that has been saved to a different folder, you need to enter the full path. I find it easier to click on **File** > **Open...** to search for where I stored that dataset on my computer if it is not stored in the working directory.

3.1 What OLS regression can tell us

This section provides a basis to compare logistic regression with OLS regression. Feel free to skip to section 3.2 if you have experience with OLS regression.

Some researchers believe that OLS regression assumes a normally distributed dependent variable, but this is not true. The assumption is that the residuals are normally distributed. There are several ways to test the distribution of the residuals. However, when the sample size is small, there is insufficient power to test the normality of the distribution of residuals. When the sample size is large, trivial violations of normality lead to small p-values (and rejection of normality) with these tests. The assumption of normally distributed residuals is helpful but not essential (Wooldridge 2010). OLS regression produces valid estimates of the regression coefficients regardless of the distribution of the residuals. However, the estimated p-values for coefficients and confidence intervals may be sensitive to violations.

It is helpful to examine the distribution of the residuals, so let's take a look at our `lbw_working.dta` example.

If we model the newborn's birthweight in grams, `bwt`, the assumption of normally distributed residuals appears reasonable. Here we want to predict the birthweight of the newborn based on

1. whether the mother was a smoker during her pregnancy (binary; `smoke`);
2. the mother's weight at her last menstruation (quantitative; `lwt`), included to remove the weight gained during pregnancy, which varies widely from mother to mother; and
3. whether the mother has a history of hypertension (binary; `ht`).

To run a conventional regression, we use the command `regress` followed by the outcome variable and a list of independent variables. The predictors are whether the mother was a smoker during pregnancy (`i.smoke`), her weight during her last menstruation (`c.lwt`), and whether she has a history of hypertension (`i.ht`). Note that we use the prefix `i.` for `smoke` and `ht`. The `i.` is an indicator that these predictors are categorical.[1] We use the prefix `c.` for `lwt` because `lwt` is a quantitative variable.

The `i.` makes the category with the lowest code the base level (reference group). The `i.` prefix is critical if we have a categorical variable with three or more levels. Stata assumes that predictors are quantitative and results will differ for categorical variables with three or more levels if the `i.` is omitted. For binary variables, omitting the `i.` will lead to the same regression result, but postestimation commands rely on the `i.` even for binary variables.[2]

We add three options after the comma following the `regress` command. The `beta` option reports the estimated standardized regression coefficients (βs). The `vsquish` option drops unnecessary blank lines in the results. The `baselevels` option will indicate the base level used for categorical independent variables (clarified below). This will become clear when we go through the results.

1. Stata documentation refers to categorical variables as factor variables and to `i.` as factor-variable notation.
2. I like to include the `i.` and `c.` notation because they clarify which variables are categorical and which are quantitative (see box 3.1). This is a helpful reminder when working with commands that are a few weeks or months old. Otherwise, I would not know whether a variable like `ht` was categorical or quantitative.

Here is the command for and the results of the OLS regression model predicting the newborn's birthweight, bwt:

```
. regress bwt i.smoke c.lwt i.ht, beta baselevels vsquish

      Source |       SS           df       MS      Number of obs   =       189
-------------+----------------------------------   F(3, 185)       =      7.16
       Model |  10391709.4         3  3463903.13   Prob > F        =    0.0001
    Residual |  89523589.2       185  483911.293   R-squared       =    0.1040
-------------+----------------------------------   Adj R-squared   =    0.0895
       Total |  99915298.6       188  531464.354   Root MSE        =    695.64

------------------------------------------------------------------------------
         bwt | Coefficient  Std. err.      t    P>|t|                     Beta
-------------+----------------------------------------------------------------
       smoke |
   Nonsmoker |          0  (base)                                            0
      Smoker |  -263.9154   103.8024    -2.54   0.012                -.1771669
         lwt |   5.350703   1.709766     3.13   0.002                 .2244101
          ht |
          No |          0  (base)                                            0
         Yes |  -586.2308   213.6239    -2.74   0.007                 -.196607
       _cons |    2390.21   230.4124    10.37   0.000                        .
------------------------------------------------------------------------------
```

The top-right section of the results reports the number of observations ($N = 189$), the model F test ($F_{3,185} = 7.16$), the corresponding p-value ($p = 0.0001$), and the R^2 (0.104). The overall model test of whether all coefficients are 0 has a p-value of less than 0.001, and the three predictors explain 10.4% of the variance in birthweight. In the central part of the results, we see that all regression coefficients have small p-values under the column labeled `P>|t|`. Under the column labeled `Coefficient`, we see that `Smoker` has an estimated coefficient (B) of -263.915, meaning that birthweights of newborns of mothers who smoke are expected to be 263.915 grams lower than the birthweights of newborns of mothers who do not smoke (base level) controlling for `lwt` and `ht`. Notice that the `Nonsmoker` category is the base level for the `smoke` variable. This is signified by the 0.

Although smoking has a sizable negative effect, the observed effect of hypertension is even more substantial. Hypertension (`Yes`) has a coefficient B of -586.231 grams (almost 21 ounces). This implies that the expected birthweight of newborns whose mothers have hypertension is 586.231 grams lower than the expected birthweight of the base-level group of mothers who do not report hypertension.

Because `smoke` and `ht` are binary variables, it makes little sense to consider their βs reported in the `Beta` column because `smoke` and `ht` have values only of 0 or 1. Remember that a β weight is how much of a standard deviation the outcome differs for a 1-standard-deviation difference in the predictor. A mother cannot be 1 standard deviation higher or lower on `smoke` and `ht` because they are measured using codes of 0 and 1. Thus, the β weights are inappropriate. I appreciate that some publications try to interpret them as measuring the effect size of categorical variables, but it makes more sense to me to assess the effect of categorical variables using the Bs than the βs. A rarely used alternative to β when you have a binary predictor is the semipartial correlation.

A useful postestimation command to run after the `regress` command is `margins`, which produces additional information beyond the Bs and βs. Because our focus is on the effects of smoking, we enter `margins` followed by `i.smoke`:

```
. margins i.smoke
Predictive margins                                   Number of obs = 189
Model VCE: OLS

Expression: Linear prediction, predict()

------------------------------------------------------------------------------
             |            Delta-method
             |     Margin   std. err.      t    P>|t|     [95% conf. interval]
-------------+----------------------------------------------------------------
       smoke |
   Nonsmoker |   3047.618   64.90121    46.96   0.000     2919.576    3175.659
      Smoker |   2783.702   80.92953    34.40   0.000     2624.039    2943.366
------------------------------------------------------------------------------
```

When the outcome variable is quantitative, as in this example, the `margins` command reports the following:

1. The estimated mean is under the `Margin` column, which adjusts for covariates.
2. With conventional OLS regression, we expect that the mean birthweight of newborns of smokers will be 2,783.702 grams (6.14 pounds) compared with newborns of nonsmoking mothers, who will have an expected mean birthweight of 3,047.618 grams (6.72 pounds). Both averages are well within a normal-birthweight range.
3. The columns labeled `t` and `P>|t|` are not useful here. They compare the expected mean birthweight with a birthweight of 0 grams rather than the difference in birthweight between the newborn of a mother who smoked and the newborn of a mother who did not smoke. No newborn will weigh exactly 0 grams.
4. The `margins` table does not show a p-value for whether the means are different. We already know that the expected means of the two groups are different because $B = -263.915$ grams, $p = 0.012$ from the regression result.
5. The last two columns report the 95% confidence interval for the estimated means.

The `margins` command means may be more valuable than the regression coefficients ($B = -263.915$ and $\beta = -0.177$). `margins` gives us their actual estimated mean birthweights.

Next we will look at our quantitative variable, mothers' weight. How important is this predictor? $\beta = 0.224$ indicates that it has a small effect. If a mother weighs 1 standard deviation more (30.575 pounds more), her newborn is expected to weigh 0.224 standard deviations more, or 163 grams (under six ounces). A rule of thumb is that a β of 0.2 is a small effect.

Looking back at the output from our **regress** command, what does $B = 5.351$, $p = 0.002$ for **lwt** indicate? If a mother weighs one pound more, her newborn is expected to weigh 5.351 grams more. This effect sounds trivial, but so is a one-pound difference in the mother's weight. What about a more meaningful difference, say, 20 pounds? Even with this difference, her newborn is expected to weigh $B = 5.351 \times 20 = 107.02$ grams more (less than 3.8 ounces). It appears that the mother's weight has little influence.

Using a linear combination, we can estimate the p-value and confidence interval for a 20-pound difference or any other difference. We use the **lincom** command for this.

```
. lincom lwt*20
 ( 1)  20*lwt = 0
```

bwt	Coefficient	Std. err.	t	P>|t|	[95% conf.	interval]
(1)	107.0141	34.19532	3.13	0.002	39.55112	174.477

Although the test for the coefficient on **lwt** has a small p-value, the effect is not substantial even for a 20-pound difference in the mother's weight. Although the confidence interval does not cross 0, it is very wide. When we move to logistic regression, interpreting the practical significance of a quantitative predictor is a more complicated process than what we have done here (see sections 6.3 and 10.4.2).

We have evaluated the effect of each predictor in the linear regression model. Recall that these inferences are based on the assumption that residuals are normally distributed.

After fitting a model with **regress**, we can use the **predict** command with the **residuals** option to generate a new variable, **resid**, that contains the residual for each observation.

```
. predict resid, residuals
```

Then we use the histogram command to create a histogram for the resid variable, that is, the residuals. The freq option shows the frequency distribution rather than the density distribution. The normal option overlays a plot of a normal distribution.

```
. histogram resid, freq normal
(bin=13, start=-2064.8013, width=308.18884)
```

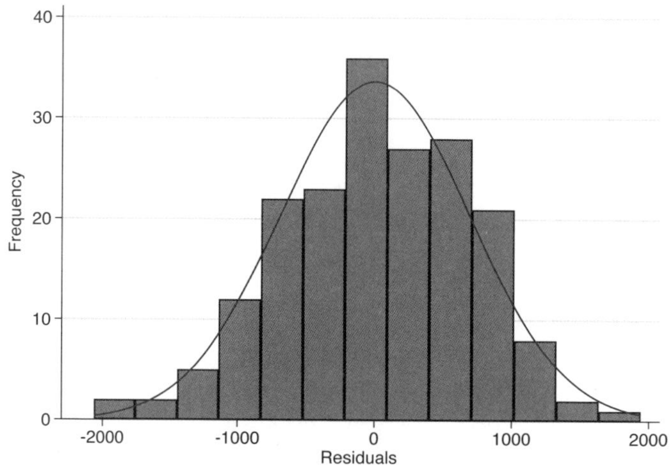

Figure 3.1. Distribution of residuals from model predicting birthweight

Figure 3.1 shows that the residuals are approximately normally distributed.

The results we have seen from this OLS regression do not help us understand the risk of clinically low birthweight associated with smoking. The newborns of mothers who smoked and mothers who did not smoke both have estimated mean birthweights that are well above the standard for low birthweight (under 2,500 grams). Even though a mother being a smoker results in a lower expected birthweight for her newborn, the estimated mean will not do a lot to convince an expecting mother to quit smoking.

We can run logistic regression predicting low birthweight to answer our research questions: If a mother is a smoker, is her newborn more at risk of being classified as having low birthweight? What is the risk of a low-birthweight newborn for mothers who are smokers and for mothers who are nonsmokers?

3.2 What logistic regression can tell us

Logistic regression uses the generalized linear model (GLM) and estimates parameters using maximum likelihood estimation rather than OLS. Essentially, it iteratively converges on the solution for the estimates that maximize the likelihood of our observed sample relationships. The GLM is much more flexible than OLS because it can fit models with different types of outcome variables (continuous, binary, multinomial, counts, etc.). A GLM can use the proper family (Gaussian, inverse Gaussian, binomial, negative binomial, Poisson, or gamma). Additionally, GLMs can use the appropriate link function (identity, logit, log, probit, or others).

A GLM for a quantitative outcome typically uses the Gaussian (normal) family with the identity link and assumes that the dependent variable is continuous with normally distributed residuals. The `regress` command and the corresponding `glm` command using maximum likelihood estimation, along with the Gaussian family and identity link, yield the same coefficient estimates.

Logistic regression is one type of GLM. It uses the binomial family and a logit link. For logistic regression, we are ultimately interested in predicting the probability of the outcome. The GLM with a logit link does not model this probability directly. Instead, it models the logit. Fortunately, we can transform the estimated logit into the estimated probability (risk). Here is an example of a GLM command, `glm`, for logistic regression:

```
. glm low i.smoke c.lwt i.ht, family(binomial) link(logit) eform
  (output omitted)
```

In addition to specifying the `family()` and `link()` options, we have added the `eform` option. This transforms the Bs to ORs for each predictor. Chapter 4 provides a detailed explanation of the meaning and interpretation of an OR. We will see that the ORs are more easily understood than the Bs, especially for a nontechnical audience. The regression coefficients for predicting the logit can also be used to get estimated probabilities of the outcome using the `margins` command (see chapter 10).

Stata has simplified the use of GLMs via a series of specific commands that implement the most common GLM applications. For logistic regression, Stata has two commands (see box 3.1).

Box 3.1. Stata's **logistic** and **logit** commands

The logistic regression command, `logistic`, reports the odds ratio (OR) for each independent variable. If we just want to estimate the logit coefficient rather than the OR, we use the `logit` command. An alternative way to obtain the logit regression coefficients is to add an option to the `logistic` command. Note that we can specify the `coef` option and get the same results as the `logit` command. Thus, the following two commands will have the same coefficients:

```
. logit low i.smoke c.lwt i.ht, vsquish baselevels
. logistic low i.smoke c.lwt i.ht, vsquish baselevels coef
```

Similarly, if we use the `logit` command, we can get the ORs directly by adding the `or` option. Thus,

```
. logit low i.smoke c.lwt i.ht, vsquish baselevels or
```

will produce the same result as the following `logistic` command:

```
. logistic low i.smoke c.lwt i.ht, vsquish baselevels
```

The `logit` command estimates the *B*s:

```
. logit low i.smoke c.lwt i.ht, vsquish baselevels
Iteration 0:  Log likelihood =   -117.336
Iteration 1:  Log likelihood =  -108.6555
Iteration 2:  Log likelihood = -108.44217
Iteration 3:  Log likelihood = -108.44138
Iteration 4:  Log likelihood = -108.44138
Logistic regression                                     Number of obs =    189
                                                        LR chi2(3)    =  17.79
                                                        Prob > chi2   = 0.0005
Log likelihood = -108.44138                             Pseudo R2     = 0.0758

------------------------------------------------------------------------------
         low | Coefficient  Std. err.      z    P>|z|     [95% conf. interval]
-------------+----------------------------------------------------------------
       smoke |
   Nonsmoker |          0  (base)
      Smoker |   .6837394    .330934     2.07   0.039     .0351206    1.332358
         lwt |  -.0180193    .006563    -2.75   0.006    -.0308825   -.005156
          ht |
          No |          0  (base)
         Yes |   1.820932   .6858989     2.65   0.008     .4765953     3.16527
       _cons |   1.080418   .8341497     1.30   0.195    -.5544857    2.715321
------------------------------------------------------------------------------
```

Many publications report only these Bs and their p-values. If the p-value is small, say, less than 0.05, they report that the variable has a significant effect. A small p-value needs to be evaluated in terms of practical significance. For instance, in a publication using logistic regression, we might read that a mother smoking significantly increases the likelihood of having a low-birthweight newborn because the coefficient is positive and the p-value is small. We should be wary of statements like this and always evaluate the practical effect.

There is some information missing from this report. How strong is the effect? What additional risk or reduction in risk does smoking contribute? Especially with large samples, a coefficient may have a small p-value without practical significance. Far too many publications need clarification of how strong the effect is. In chapter 4, we will see how difficult it is for most audiences to judge the practical significance of a B for a logistic regression model.

The `logistic` command can help us make our report more informative. It is an alternative to `logit` that runs `logit` in the background and transforms the Bs into ORs:

```
. logistic low i.smoke c.lwt i.ht, vsquish baselevels
Logistic regression                                     Number of obs =    189
                                                        LR chi2(3)    =  17.79
                                                        Prob > chi2   = 0.0005
Log likelihood = -108.44138                             Pseudo R2     = 0.0758

------------------------------------------------------------------------------
         low | Odds ratio   Std. err.      z    P>|z|     [95% conf. interval]
-------------+----------------------------------------------------------------
       smoke |
   Nonsmoker |          1  (base)
      Smoker |   1.981273   .6556705     2.07   0.039     1.035745     3.78997
         lwt |   .9821421   .0064458    -2.75   0.006     .9695895    .9948572
          ht |
          No |          1  (base)
         Yes |   6.177616    4.23722     2.65   0.008     1.610582    23.69513
       _cons |    2.94591    2.45733     1.30   0.195     .5743676    15.10946
------------------------------------------------------------------------------
Note: _cons estimates baseline odds.
```

The OR appears under the column `Odds ratio`. The ORs express the strength of a relationship. We will get into the model more later, but let us focus now on what a mother's smoking means for her newborn's odds of a low birthweight controlling for the covariates. The OR is 1 for nonsmokers (base level) and 1.981 for smokers. An OR of 1.0 is like an OLS regression B of 0. Multiplying the odds by 1.0 has no effect. If the mother smokes during pregnancy, the odds of her newborn having a clinically low birthweight are nearly double that of the odds if the mother does not smoke. The odds of a clinically low-birthweight newborn are multiplied by 1.981, $p = 0.039$. This doubling of the odds contrasts with the mothers in the base level who are nonsmokers. Importantly, this OR is controlling for the other predictors. Reporting this result to a woman planning to have a baby should make her rethink any thoughts of smoking! The mother more readily understands OR $= 1.981$, $p = 0.039$ (nearly doubling the odds) than $B = 0.684$, $p = 0.039$.

Note that an OR of 2 does not mean a doubled probability or risk of having a low-birthweight newborn but rather that the odds nearly double. This can be misleading if the outcome is a rare event, such as the mother dying during childbirth. If smoking doubled the odds of death, the event would still be rare. ORs are more easily understood than the regression coefficients that predict logits, but remember that the ORs do not directly measure the difference in risk, which comes from comparing the probability of low birthweight for smokers and nonsmokers. We will see much more on estimating the probability in chapter 10.

In the following chapters of this book, you will learn more about the OR and alternatives that may be better.

3.2.1 Robust and cluster–robust estimation

Most Stata regression commands, including `logit` and `logistic`, have a `vce()` option available to specify the type of standard errors reported. `vce(robust)` and `vce(cluster` *clustvar*`)` are two of the available options for estimating robust and cluster–robust standard errors, respectively.

Let us examine two situations where we might add the `vce()` option, which estimates the standard errors and resulting p-values of parameters differently. The first situation is when we have an imperfect model. Perhaps a relevant predictor was unavailable—many publications using logistic regression leave out relevant predictors. Thankfully, a model may still be useful even if it is imperfect.

The second situation is when we have a clustered sample. Here is a hypothetical example. Our total sample includes 100 cases from each of 10 hospitals for a total of 1,000 cases. Each hospital is a cluster of cases. We need to adjust for the possibility that each cluster of 100 cases is more homogeneous than the same number of randomly selected cases from the combined instances of all 10 hospitals.

An imperfect model

We rarely know if our specification of the model is the one valid specification. Indeed, there are other predictors of low birthweight. We have included some crucial predictors, but what about the mother's diet during pregnancy? Her household income? The effect of smoking might be less dramatic if we included those additional covariates. An alternative problem is including variables that have no independent effect on the risk of low birthweight. These would add noise to our model.

Without a perfect model specification, we can use a robust estimator of the standard errors. It is essential to note that this does not eliminate any bias in the parameter estimates themselves, which remain unchanged when a robust estimator is used. Bill Sribney, formerly of StataCorp, wrote, "Sometimes one just has to live with missing predictors and badly fitting models because data were collected for only a few predictors. In this case, I'd use the robust variance estimator." (See https://www.stata.com/support/faqs/statistics/robust-variance-estimator/.) The robust estimator changes the estimated standard error, *p*-value, and confidence interval but not the *B* or OR.

Let us compare our original default with what happens with a robust estimator. We will do this for the *B*s rather than the ORs (the *p*-values are identical for both *B*s and ORs):

1. Run the `logit` command.
2. Run the `estimates store` command for this solution, calling it `Base`.
3. Run the `logit` command with robust standard errors using the `vce(robust)` option.
4. Run the `estimates store` command for this solution, calling it `Robust`.
5. Run an `estimates table` command showing both sets of estimates.

Here are the first four commands:

```
. logit low i.smoke
. estimates store Base
. logit low i.smoke, vce(robust)
. estimates store Robust
```

We run the `estimates store` command immediately after each logistic regression and name it. The `estimates table` command has optional formatting for the standard errors and their probabilities. Entering `se(%8.4f)` tells Stata to use a fixed format with eight spaces for each standard error, keeping four decimal places. Notice that the standard errors have four digits after the decimal place. Entering `p(%4.3f)` tells Stata to use a fixed p-value format with four spaces, three of which are after the decimal.

```
. estimates table Base Robust, se(%8.4f) p(%4.3f)
```

Variable	Base	Robust
smoke		
Smoker	.70405921	.70405921
	0.3196	0.3205
	0.028	0.028
_cons	-1.0870515	-1.0870515
	0.2147	0.2153
	0.000	0.000

Legend: b/se/p

The Bs are identical whether or not we use the robust estimator. The ORs are not shown but they are also identical. Specifying the `vce(robust)` option affects only how the standard errors are estimated. The standard errors are slightly different—0.3196 versus 0.3205 for `smoke`. This difference is too small for the p's to differ when rounded to three decimal places. The robust estimator typically has larger standard errors, which results in larger p-values.

Clustered sample design

Many surveys use cluster sampling. To generalize to the population, we need to adjust the estimation of standard errors. The cases selected from within each cluster are correlated because they are more homogeneous than the same number chosen independently from the larger population. For example, one hospital might serve an upper-middle-class area that is 90% White, non-Hispanic, while another might serve a low-income area that is 70% Hispanic. This means that cases from each hospital will be more homogeneous than those drawn independently from the general population. This violates the assumption that all cases are sampled independently. The most effective way to handle complex sample designs is by employing Stata's `svy` prefix command with the appropriate sample design specifications (see the *Stata Survey Data Reference Manual*). The `svy` prefix can account for clustering and adjust for the varying proportions of each subsample. For instance, when sampling 300 students from each of the four high schools, one must consider the relative sizes of the high schools. Further discussion of the `svy` prefix command is beyond the scope of this book.

Here we will show how to adjust standard errors for clustering by using a sandwich estimator of the variance–covariance matrix. Open `hospid1.dta`:

```
. webuse hospid1, clear
```

This includes an identification variable, `hospid`, for each of the 20 hospitals from which data were collected. We use the `fre` command (introduced in chapter 2) with this variable:

```
. fre hospid
hospid — Hospital ID
```

		Freq.	Percent	Valid	Cum.
Valid	1	14	7.41	7.41	7.41
	2	21	11.11	11.11	18.52
	3	19	10.05	10.05	28.57
	4	8	4.23	4.23	32.80
	5	4	2.12	2.12	34.92
	6	8	4.23	4.23	39.15
	7	11	5.82	5.82	44.97
	8	10	5.29	5.29	50.26
	9	6	3.17	3.17	53.44
	10	6	3.17	3.17	56.61
	11	7	3.70	3.70	60.32
	12	4	2.12	2.12	62.43
	13	12	6.35	6.35	68.78
	14	8	4.23	4.23	73.02
	15	10	5.29	5.29	78.31
	16	12	6.35	6.35	84.66
	17	4	2.12	2.12	86.77
	18	7	3.70	3.70	90.48
	19	8	4.23	4.23	94.71
	20	10	5.29	5.29	100.00
	Total	189	100.00	100.00	

We will run the logistic regression first without any adjustment and then with an adjustment so that we can compare the results:

```
. logit low i.race i.smoke i.ht, baselevels
  (output omitted)
. estimates store nocluster
. logit low i.race i.smoke i.ht, baselevels vce(cluster hospid)
  (output omitted)
. estimates store cluster
```

We do not present the results of the two logistic regressions, but we will provide a table comparing their estimated *B*s, standard errors, and *p*-values. In the following command, we specify how the standard errors should be reported using `se(%8.4f)` and how the *p*-values should be reported using `p(%4.3f)`.

```
. estimates table nocluster cluster, se(%8.4f) p(%4.3f)
```

Variable	nocluster	cluster
race		
Black	1.0308057	1.0308057
	0.4971	0.5828
	0.038	0.077
Other	1.1201812	1.1201812
	0.4046	0.2942
	0.006	0.000
smoke		
1	1.1296627	1.1296627
	0.3733	0.3285
	0.002	0.001
ht		
1	1.1795455	1.1795455
	0.6236	0.6026
	0.059	0.050
_cons	-1.9314496	-1.9314496
	0.3628	0.2397
	0.000	0.000

Legend: b/se/p

Please note that our adjustment applies only to the standard errors and the resulting *p*-values. The logistic regression *B*s and ORs (not shown) remain identical whether or not we use a robust estimator. Robust estimators of the standard errors generally produce larger standard errors when cases within clusters are highly correlated. When the clusters are very homogeneous, the impact on the *p*-values can be dramatic. With this dataset, the effects are minor.

4 Interpreting an odds ratio

4.1 What is an odds ratio?

So far, we have used the term "odds ratio" (OR) loosely. Let us now be specific about its meaning. First, let us create a table for odds of a mother having a low-birthweight newborn by whether she is a smoker. This bivariate relationship will have different results than our logistic regression command because we are not controlling for covariates. We use the `tabulate` command, entering our outcome variable (`low`) first followed by our independent variable (`smoke`). The variable we list first will be the row variable, and the variable we list last will be the column variable. We add the `column` option so that Stata reports the percentages for each column. This helps us determine if mothers who are smokers have higher odds of a low-birthweight newborn than mothers who are not smokers.

```
. use "lbw_working"
(Hosmer & Lemeshow data)
. tabulate low smoke, column

+-------------------+
| Key               |
|-------------------|
|     frequency     |
| column percentage |
+-------------------+

           |     Smoked during
Birthweigh |       pregnancy
  t<2500g  | Nonsmoker     Smoker |     Total
-----------+----------------------+----------
        No |        86         44 |       130 
           |     74.78      59.46 |     68.78 
-----------+----------------------+----------
       Yes |        29         30 |        59 
           |     25.22      40.54 |     31.22 
-----------+----------------------+----------
     Total |       115         74 |       189 
           |    100.00     100.00 |    100.00 
```

Second, we calculate the odds of having a low-birthweight newborn for smokers and nonsmokers. These odds for the 74 smokers are the number who have a low-birthweight newborn (30) over the number who have a normal-birthweight newborn (44). Notice that we are not calculating the *risk* of these smokers having a low-birthweight newborn. The risk is $30/74 = 0.405$. By contrast, the *odds* are

$$\text{Odds of low-birthweight newborn for smokers} = 30/44 = 0.682$$

Because the odds are less than 1.0, smokers have fewer low-birthweight newborns than they do normal-birthweight newborns.

What about nonsmokers? The odds of a low-birthweight newborn for the 115 nonsmokers are the number of mothers who have a low-birthweight newborn (29) over the number who do not (86).

$$\text{Odds of low-birthweight newborn for nonsmokers} = 29/86 = 0.337$$

The odds of a low-birthweight newborn for smokers are slightly more than double the odds for nonsmokers: 0.682 versus 0.337.

We calculate the OR by comparing these odds. Note that we need to put the odds for smokers on top because smokers are coded as 1 for `smoke`.

$$\text{OR} = \frac{\text{Odds for smokers (code} = 1)}{\text{Odds for nonsmokers (code} = 0)} = \frac{0.682}{0.337} = 2.024$$

In this example, we have not controlled for other independent variables. This OR differs from the one that accounts for control variables, as in section 3.2, where the OR is 1.981.

Instead of calculating the OR by hand, we could use the `logistic` command with the single predictor `smoke`.

```
. logistic low i.smoke, baselevels vsquish
Logistic regression                                     Number of obs =    189
                                                        LR chi2(1)    =   4.87
                                                        Prob > chi2   = 0.0274
Log likelihood = -114.9023                              Pseudo R2     = 0.0207

------------------------------------------------------------------------------
         low | Odds ratio   Std. err.      z    P>|z|     [95% conf. interval]
-------------+----------------------------------------------------------------
       smoke |
   Nonsmoker |          1  (base)
      Smoker |   2.021944   .6462989     2.20   0.028      1.08066    3.783112
       _cons |   .3372093   .0724103    -5.06   0.000     .2213694    .5136667
------------------------------------------------------------------------------
Note: _cons estimates baseline odds.
```

The above output shows an OR of 2.022. It also reports $z = 2.20$, $p = 0.028$. The slight difference between the ORs of 2.022 and 2.024, which we calculated by hand, is due to a rounding error in our hand calculations. Stata commands use double precision in all calculations, which helps avoid such errors. The essential advantages of estimating the OR using the `logistic` command are that `logistic` provides a p-value and confidence interval and allows us to control for covariates.

One major limitation of the OR is that it is often misinterpreted as a relative risk (RR) (see section 15.4). Looking back at the table, we see that 30/74 or 40.54% of the mothers who were smokers had a newborn with a low birthweight compared with just 25.22% of the mothers who were not smokers. Thus, the RR is

$$\text{RR} = \frac{40.54}{25.22} = 1.607$$

Careful interpretation of each type of statistic is important. News writers, public speakers, and even some researchers sometimes misinterpret the OR as a measure of the RR (see section 15.3).

4.2 Interpreting ORs as a percentage difference for binary predictors

Hopefully, you understand that an OR greater than 1.0 indicates increased odds and that an OR less than 1.0 indicates decreased odds. Beginners may need help interpreting ORs that are below 1.0.

Sometimes, it is helpful to think of the OR in terms of the percentage difference in the odds for a one-point difference in the score for a predictor. When an OR is greater than 1.0, we calculate

$$\text{Percentage difference} = (\text{OR} - 1.0) \times 100\%$$

The percentage increase is $(2.02 - 1.0) \times 100\% = 102\%$. Thus, the odds of a low-birthweight newborn for a mother who smoked are 102% higher than the odds for a mother who did not smoke.

What about an OR that is less than 1.0? Interpreting such an OR as a percentage drop in the odds is useful. Suppose that we want to know if being White reduces the odds of high blood pressure. We do not have `white` as a variable, but we do have a variable named `race` that has three categories. We can use the `fre` command from chapter 2 to display these categories:

```
. fre race

race — Race

                    |   Freq.    Percent      Valid       Cum.
--------------------+--------------------------------------------
Valid   1 White     |      96      50.79      50.79      50.79
        2 Black     |      26      13.76      13.76      64.55
        3 Other     |      67      35.45      35.45     100.00
        Total       |     189     100.00     100.00
```

We will recode the race variable to generate the white variable. The following recode command extends over more than a single line, so we use a blank space and three hash marks (///) to tell Stata that the next line is part of the command (see box 6.1):

```
. recode race (1 = 1 "White") (2 = 0 "Other") (3 = 0 "Other"), ///
> generate(white)
(93 differences between race and white)
```

Now we can run logistic regression using white to predict low:

```
. logistic low i.white, baselevels vsquish
Logistic regression                                     Number of obs =    189
                                                        LR chi2(1)    =   4.81
                                                        Prob > chi2   = 0.0282
Log likelihood = -114.92867                             Pseudo R2     = 0.0205

------------------------------------------------------------------------------
         low | Odds ratio   Std. err.      z    P>|z|     [95% conf. interval]
-------------+----------------------------------------------------------------
       white |
       Other |          1  (base)
       White |   .4988585   .1597115    -2.17   0.030     .2663556     .934314
       _cons |   .6315789   .1344561    -2.16   0.031     .4161179    .9586033
------------------------------------------------------------------------------
Note: _cons estimates baseline odds.
```

We see that White has an OR $= 0.499$, $p = 0.03$. Because the OR is less than 1.0, to interpret it as a percentage difference, we use

$$\text{Percentage difference} = (1 - \text{OR}) \times 100\%$$

Thus, the percentage reduction in the odds is estimated to be $(1.0 - 0.499) \times 100\% = 50.1\%$. Mothers who are White have 50.1% lower odds of having a low-birthweight newborn than mothers who are not White.

A valid interpretation of the OR is more complex for quantitative independent variables. Consider the OR of 0.982 for the mother's weight (lwt) at her last menstruation (see section 3.2). The more she weighed, the lower her odds of having a low-birthweight newborn. Because the OR is less than 1.0, we calculate $(1.0 - 0.982) \times 100\% = 1.8\%$ reduction in odds. Thus, the odds of a low-birthweight newborn are 1.8% lower for each additional pound the mother weighed at her last menstruation. This does not sound like a big percentage difference, nor does a one-pound difference in the mother's weight.

What about a substantial weight difference, say, a difference of 1 standard deviation? A standard-deviation difference in lwt is 30.575 pounds (using the summarize lwt command). How do we calculate the OR for a 30.575-pound difference in the mother's weight? Unlike conventional ordinary least-squares regression using a quantitative predictor, with logistic regression, we must *not* multiply the change in weight by the OR $= 0.982 \times 30.575 = 30.025$ to calculate the OR for a 1-standard-deviation difference in the mother's weight.

Later, in section 6.3, I will explain how to estimate the OR for a difference of 1 standard deviation (or any specific difference) in a quantitative independent variable. Section 6.3 will show the estimated OR of a low-birthweight newborn for 1 standard deviation and a higher mother's weight at her last menstruation. The $\text{OR}_{\text{oneSd}} = 0.595$, $p = 0.030$. Thus, a substantial difference in mother's weight has a strong effect on the OR.

When we predicted the newborn's birthweight (`bwt`), we got very different results than when we predicted whether the newborn would have a clinically low birthweight (`low`). We found that the mother's weight had a weak or negligible effect on the newborn's birthweight. By contrast, predicting the probability of a clinically low-birthweight newborn shows that the mother's weight was a strong predictor.

5 What is wrong with ordinary least-squares regression for a binary outcome?

5.1 Hypothetical data

Suppose that we want to predict the probability of heterosexual couples getting divorced within their first five years of marriage. We will create hypothetical data with 20 observations. The couples who got divorced in their first five years of marriage are coded as 1, and couples who were still married after five years are coded as 0. We predict the probability of divorce, that is, 1. Shortly before getting married, each couple was observed for 10 minutes discussing how many children they wanted, if any. Observers counted the number of positive statements the man made about his future wife. We will use the number of positive comments made by the man to predict whether the couple will get divorced within the first five years of marriage.

We can input a small dataset like this directly. First, we need to clear any open dataset. (Remember to save the open dataset if you have changed it.) We use the `input` command followed by a list of the variable names. We enter the individual values separated by a blank space. For example, the first couple has scores of 1 for `id`, 0 for `divorced`, and 8 for `positives`. The 19th couple has scores of 19 for `id`, 1 for `divorced`, and 0 for `positives`. We use a closing `end` command once we have entered all the data. Here is how we create our hypothetical dataset:

```
. input id divorced positives
                id    divorced   positives
  1. 1 0 8
  2. 2 0 10
  3. 3 0 7
  4. 4 0 7
  5. 5 0 8
  6. 6 0 4
  7. 7 0 10
  8. 8 0 9
  9. 9 0 7
 10. 10 1 5
 11. 11 1 1
 12. 12 1 4
 13. 13 1 2
 14. 14 1 3
 15. 15 1 4
 16. 16 1 7
 17. 17 1 3
 18. 18 1 4
 19. 19 1 0
 20. 20 1 1
 21. end
```

Below, we list the hypothetical data for divorces within the first five years by number of positive comments:

```
. list id divorced positives

     +-----------------------------+
     | id   divorced   positi~s    |
     |-----------------------------|
  1. |  1          0          8    |
  2. |  2          0         10    |
  3. |  3          0          7    |
  4. |  4          0          7    |
  5. |  5          0          8    |
     |-----------------------------|
  6. |  6          0          4    |
  7. |  7          0         10    |
  8. |  8          0          9    |
  9. |  9          0          7    |
 10. | 10          1          5    |
     |-----------------------------|
 11. | 11          1          1    |
 12. | 12          1          4    |
 13. | 13          1          2    |
 14. | 14          1          3    |
 15. | 15          1          4    |
     |-----------------------------|
 16. | 16          1          7    |
 17. | 17          1          3    |
 18. | 18          1          4    |
 19. | 19          1          0    |
 20. | 20          1          1    |
     +-----------------------------+
```

5.2 How does logistic regression fit better than ordinary least-squares linear regression?

We can fit a model for being divorced using either linear regression or logistic regression. To see why logistic regression is advantageous, we compare the raw data with predictions from both linear and logistic regression models

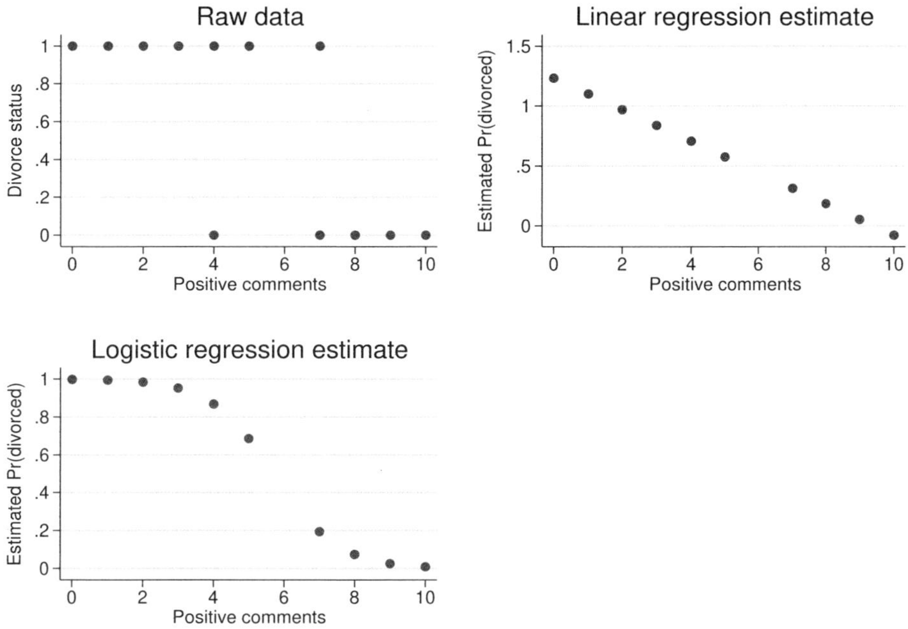

Figure 5.1. Scatterplot comparing linear and logistic regressions with raw data

The upper left of figure 5.1 shows a scatterplot between divorces within the first five years and the number of positive statements using the raw data we just entered. Notice that every man who made fewer than four positive comments during the discussion was divorced within five years. By contrast, nearly every man who made more than six positive comments was still married after five years. What about those men who made four to six positive comments? For them, the results were mixed: some were still married and some were divorced. We can think of this part of the bivariate distribution as a "zone of transition". We generated hypothetical data for an extreme example, but with binary outcomes with strong quantitative predictors, we typically see these three zones. One zone will have all or most cases that have outcome 1. A second zone will have all or most cases that have outcome 0. A third zone, the zone of transition, will have mixed results.

Immediately to the right of the raw data in figure 5.1 is the estimated probability of divorce using ordinary least-squares (OLS) linear regression. There are two problems with OLS linear regression in addition to violating assumptions of a continuous outcome variable and a normal distribution of residuals:

1. For 1 or 2 positive statements in the 10-minute session, the conventional OLS regression predicts a probability of divorce greater than 1.0, which is impossible; this would mean that the couple is more than certain they will get divorced.
2. For 10 positive statements, the conventional OLS regression predicts a probability of less than 0.0, which is also impossible; there cannot be less than no chance of a divorce.

Linear regression relies on an identity link to predict the probability of divorce directly and forces the estimated probabilities onto a straight line, resulting in these out-of-range predicted values.

Logistic regression predicts a logit rather than the raw score. We explain this in box 5.1 and in more detail in chapter 6. When we transform the predicted logit into a predicted probability, it becomes a curve (see the lower plot in figure 5.1). The curve for the logistic regression always allows for the zone of transition. This is a better way to predict the risk of the couple getting divorced. There is not much change in the risk of divorce between 0 and 4 positive comments; these couples have little chance of celebrating their fifth year of marriage. However, between 4 and 7 positive comments, there is a rapid drop in the risk of divorce. Finally, the couples where the man makes between 8 and 10 positive comments have little chance of getting divorced. Those couples can safely plan how to celebrate their fifth year of marriage.

Box 5.1. How is logistic regression a linear model?

> Logistic regression uses a linear model to predict the logit, that is, the natural logarithm of the odds. The relationship between the natural logarithm of the odds and the quantitative predictor will form a straight line. However, we transform the predicted natural logarithm of the odds to estimate the probability of the outcome. The predicted probability or risk of the outcome will follow a curve allowing for the zone of transition. Our hypothetical data show an extreme curve for this zone. With actual data, the curve is typically less dramatic.

6 Fitting and interpreting logistic regression models

6.1 Interpreting coefficients and odds ratios

Publications may report just the logistic regression coefficients (Bs), just the odds ratios (ORs), or both. We interpret the Bs as follows:

> For each one-unit difference for the score of an independent variable, there is an estimated B difference in the natural logarithm of the odds (logit), holding all other independent variables constant. For example, in section 3.2, we found that for each additional pound a mother weighed at her last menstruation, the natural logarithm of the odds of having a low-birthweight newborn is estimated to be $B = -0.018$ lower.

Laypeople may be uncomfortable interpreting changes in the natural logarithms of odds. The interpretation of the Bs may be correct but is likely unclear to most end users. Reporting only those variables that are statistically significant and the direction of their effects is also inadequate. These become profoundly misleading on a large sample when even a tiny effect size will have a small p-value. Unfortunately, what is likely considered statistically significant in many cases is an effect that needs to be bigger for practical significance.

We can exponentiate the Bs to get the ORs, which are easier to interpret:

> For each one-unit difference for the score of an independent variable, the estimated odds of the outcome variable is multiplied by a factor of the OR, holding all other independent variables constant. For our example, an OR of 1.981 means that a one-unit higher score on smoking (smoking versus not smoking) approximately doubles the estimated odds of low birthweight.

If we read an article that reports only the Bs, we can convert the Bs to ORs by exponentiating the Bs. Exponentiation raises the mathematical constant e (approximately 2.71828) to the Bth power.

$$\text{OR} = e^B$$

Alternatively, we can convert an OR to a B by calculating the natural log of the OR:

$$B = \ln(\text{OR})$$

Stata's built-in calculator makes both transformations simple. Suppose that we see $B = 0.6932$, $p < 0.001$ in an article. How do we convert this to an OR? We want the value of $e^B = 2.71828^{0.6932} = 2.0001$. Stata makes this easy to calculate using the `display` command. In the Command window, we run

```
. display exp(0.6932)
2.0001056
```

To convert OR $= 2.0001$ to a B, we would run

```
. display ln(2.0001)
.69319718
```

Table 6.1 shows a range of ORs and their corresponding Bs.

Table 6.1. Regression Bs and corresponding ORs

OR	B
−1.609	0.2
−0.912	0.4
−0.511	0.6
−0.223	0.8
0.000	1.0
0.182	1.2
0.336	1.4
0.470	1.6
0.588	1.8
0.693	2.0
0.788	2.2
0.875	2.4
0.956	2.6
1.030	2.8
1.099	3.0

6.2 Fitting logistic regression models with multiple predictors

Now we fit a model with multiple quantitative and categorical predictors and consider how to interpret the results. First, we will fit the model by using `logit`, which reports the Bs.

```
. use "lbw_working"
(Hosmer & Lemeshow data)
. logit low i.smoke c.age c.lwt i.ht c.ftv i.race, ///
> baselevels vsquish
Iteration 0:  Log likelihood =   -117.336
Iteration 1:  Log likelihood = -104.34815
Iteration 2:  Log likelihood = -103.92789
Iteration 3:  Log likelihood = -103.92653
Iteration 4:  Log likelihood = -103.92653
Logistic regression                                     Number of obs =    189
                                                        LR chi2(7)    =  26.82
                                                        Prob > chi2   = 0.0004
Log likelihood = -103.92653                             Pseudo R2     = 0.1143

------------------------------------------------------------------------------
         low | Coefficient  Std. err.      z    P>|z|     [95% conf. interval]
-------------+----------------------------------------------------------------
       smoke |
   Nonsmoker |          0  (base)
     Smoker  |   1.072858   .3907013     2.75   0.006      .3070975    1.838619
         age |   -.022537   .0355025    -0.63   0.526     -.0921205    .0470466
         lwt |  -.0174205   .0068796    -2.53   0.011     -.0309042   -.0039368
          ht |
          No |          0  (base)
         Yes |   1.747546   .6924296     2.52   0.012      .3904088    3.104683
         ftv |   .0367723   .1702244     0.22   0.829     -.2968614     .370406
        race |
       White |          0  (base)
       Black |   1.242374   .5266903     2.36   0.018        .21008    2.274668
       Other |   .9297771   .4292107     2.17   0.030      .0885396    1.771015
       _cons |   .7866598   1.157127     0.68   0.497     -1.481268    3.054588
------------------------------------------------------------------------------
```

At the end of the first line in the `logit` command above is a blank space and three forward hash marks (///), which tells Stata that the command continues to the next line (see box 6.1).

Box 6.1. How does Stata know that you have reached the end of a command?

> When a command extends over more than one line in a Stata do-file, you can enter a space and three forward slashes (`///`) at the end of each line except for the last line of the command (see the do-file in appendix A for examples). Remember to put a space before the slashes; it is easy to overlook this.
>
> However, if you choose to enter the command directly in the Command window, you do not need to use the space and three slashes—just keep typing. After you are done typing the command, simply press the *Enter* or *Return* key to run the command.

For the estimation of the ORs, we use the **logistic** command:

```
. logistic low i.smoke c.age c.lwt i.ht c.ftv i.race, ///
> baselevels vsquish
Logistic regression                                     Number of obs =    189
                                                        LR chi2(7)    =  26.82
                                                        Prob > chi2   = 0.0004
Log likelihood = -103.92653                             Pseudo R2     = 0.1143

------------------------------------------------------------------------------
         low | Odds ratio   Std. err.      z    P>|z|     [95% conf. interval]
-------------+----------------------------------------------------------------
       smoke |
   Nonsmoker |          1  (base)
      Smoker |   2.923724   1.142303     2.75   0.006     1.359473    6.287846
         age |   .9777151   .0347113    -0.63   0.526     .9119952    1.048171
         lwt |   .9827303   .0067607    -2.53   0.011     .9695685    .9960709
          ht |
          No |          1  (base)
         Yes |   5.740497    3.97489     2.52   0.012     1.477585    22.30215
         ftv |   1.037457   .1766005     0.22   0.829      .743147    1.448323
        race |
       White |          1  (base)
       Black |   3.463827   1.824364     2.36   0.018     1.233777     9.72469
       Other |   2.533944   1.087596     2.17   0.030     1.092578    5.876813
       _cons |   2.196049   2.541109     0.68   0.497     .2273492    21.21244
------------------------------------------------------------------------------
Note: _cons estimates baseline odds.
```

6.3 Interpreting ORs for quantitative predictors

Interpreting ORs for quantitative predictors is more complicated with logistic regression than ordinary least-squares regression. How strong is the effect of the mother's weight at her last menstruation? The OR is 0.983. This effect is likely not attributable to chance (p-value $= 0.011$), but how do we assess its importance? With logistic regression, an OR of 1.0 signifies that the odds are multiplied by 1. That is, the predictor has no effect if the OR is 1.0. At first glance, the OR (0.983) and the B (-0.017) for the mother's weight at her last menstruation can be misinterpreted as indicating that her weight has no practical significance. The effect of `lwt` seems trivial, considering that an OR of 1.0 ($B = 0$) indicates no effect. However, remember that `lwt` ranges from 80 to 250 pounds and that the OR and B refer to the effect of a single-pound difference.

We would hardly expect a big effect on the newborns' weights when comparing one mother who weighed 144 pounds with a second mother who weighed 145 pounds. Before we discuss the strength of the effect of a mother's weight, we should decide what level of difference is substantial. We might pick a specific difference, say, 10 pounds. Another researcher might pick a 20-pound difference. In many research fields, there is a consensus that 1 standard deviation on a quantitative predictor is a substantial difference. When we ran the `summarize` command in chapter 2, we found that the standard deviation was 30.575 pounds.[1] What are the B and OR for a 1-standard-deviation difference in weight?

To calculate the OR, we multiply the B by whatever difference we decide is substantial before exponentiating. Remember, for a one-unit difference in the predictor, the OR is e^B. For a 1-standard-deviation difference in the predictor, the calculated OR is $e^{B \times \mathrm{Sd}}$. Similarly, if we decide that a 10-pound difference in weight is substantial, the adjusted OR is $e^{B \times 10}$.

Using Stata's `display` command for the 1-standard-deviation difference, we get

```
. display exp(-0.017*30.575)
.59465433
```

For a 1-standard-deviation-higher mother's weight, the OR of 0.595 means that the odds of a low-birthweight newborn will be $(1 - 0.595) \times 100 = 40.5\%$ lower. So an OR of 0.981 for a 1-pound difference may not sound like much of an effect, but a 1-standard-deviation difference in the mother's weight has a practically significant effect. If we want the OR for a 10-pound difference in the mother's weight at her last menstruation, we run

```
. display exp(-0.017*10)
.84366482
```

The p-value is unchanged.

1. This is fine because there were no missing cases. It would be better if we ran the postestimation command `estat summarize lwt`, which produces a standard deviation of 30.575. This is what we got in the last chapter when we ran `summarize` because we have no missing values. If we have missing values, we should use `estat summarize` because it drops observations that have missing values on any variables, as does the logistic regression.

Instead of calculating the effects by hand or using the `display` command, we can let Stata do the work for us by using the `lincom` command with the `or` option. After estimating the ORs for the logistic regression, we can run

```
. lincom 30.57515*lwt, or
( 1)  30.57515*[low]lwt = 0
```

low	Odds ratio	Std. err.	z	P>|z|	[95% conf.	interval]
(1)	.587056	.1234833	-2.53	0.011	.3887183	.8865926

```
. lincom 10*lwt, or
( 1)  10*[low]lwt = 0
```

low	Odds ratio	Std. err.	z	P>|z|	[95% conf.	interval]
(1)	.8401245	.0577968	-2.53	0.011	.73415	.9613964

This way, we work directly from the OR for `lwt`. We also get a 95% confidence interval for the estimates.

6.4 Selecting the right base level for categorical predictors

What about a categorical predictor with more than two levels, such as race? The base-level category, by default, is the category with the lowest code. `White` is coded as 1, `Black` is coded as 2, and `Other` is coded as 3. By default, `White` is the base level (reference group) because it has the lowest code of the three categories. Thus, the OR $= 3.464$, $p = 0.018$ for `Black` means that the estimated odds of a low-birthweight newborn for a Black mother are 3.464 times greater than those of a White mother. The `Other` category has an OR $= 2.534$, $p = 0.030$. This means that the odds of having a low-birthweight newborn for a mother classified as `Other` are 2.534 times those of a White mother.

Two points are important:

1. The comparisons of `Black` and `Other` are with `White` but not with each other. The results do not tell us whether `Black` and `Other` have different ORs (see section 14.2 or use the `contrast` command to test that difference).
2. We may want the base level to be something other than the category with the lowest code. It is essential to have a reasonable justification for the category we select when our categorical predictor has three or more response options.

What makes a good base level? We need a category that meets the following criteria:

1. It has sufficient observations to allow a stable estimate. It does not have to be the most frequent category, but it needs a large enough N to get a stable estimate for the base level. If we use a rare option as the base level, we may not have a stable base for comparison.

2. It is either a normatively or a theoretically justified base level. That is, it is the group that we want to compare with other groups.

For `race`, choosing White as the base level makes sense:

1. More than half the observations are White, so we should get a stable base estimate.

2. White is a normative case in the US because Whites are currently the largest population.

3. `White` is theoretically justified as the base level in the US because White people are the most benefited by the social structure, giving them the most capital. Because of White people's structurally advantaged position in the US, we expect them to have the lowest odds of having low-birthweight newborns.

There are models where the base-level choice could be clearer. Many questionnaires are designed such that Hispanic people are coded as 1. Consider a questionnaire that uses these response options for `race`: `Hispanic` = 1, `White` = 2, `Black` = 3, `Asian and Pacific Islander` = 4, and `Other` = 5. You might want to make `White` the base level rather than `Hispanic` because Whites are a large group and have an advantaged position in the US. Another researcher might want to keep `Hispanic` as the base level. Hispanics are a large enough group in much of the US to give you a reliable base level, but if your sample were limited to residents of Maine (under 2% Hispanic in 2021), this may not work on a small sample.

In our data, `race` is coded as 1 for `White`, 2 for `Black`, and 3 for `Other`. How do we override Stata's default and make `Black` the base level? We can do so within the `logistic` command by replacing `i.race` with `ib2.race`, where `b2` specifies that 2 (`Black`) is the base level:

```
. logistic low i.smoke c.age c.lwt i.ht c.ftv ib2.race, ///
> baselevels vsquish
Logistic regression                                     Number of obs =    189
                                                        LR chi2(7)    =  26.82
                                                        Prob > chi2   = 0.0004
Log likelihood = -103.92653                             Pseudo R2     = 0.1143

------------------------------------------------------------------------------
         low | Odds ratio   Std. err.      z    P>|z|     [95% conf. interval]
-------------+----------------------------------------------------------------
       smoke |
   Nonsmoker |          1  (base)
      Smoker |   2.923724   1.142303     2.75   0.006     1.359473    6.287846
         age |   .9777151   .0347113    -0.63   0.526     .9119952    1.048171
         lwt |   .9827303   .0067607    -2.53   0.011     .9695685    .9960709
          ht |
          No |          1  (base)
         Yes |   5.740497    3.97489     2.52   0.012     1.477585    22.30215
         ftv |   1.037457   .1766005     0.22   0.829      .743147    1.448323
        race |
       White |    .288698   .1520545    -2.36   0.018      .102831    .8105194
       Black |          1  (base)
       Other |   .7315447   .3927675    -0.58   0.560      .255405     2.09533
       _cons |   7.606733   9.294297     1.66   0.097     .6936756    83.41419
------------------------------------------------------------------------------
Note: _cons estimates baseline odds.
```

Now the reported odds ratios are for comparisons of `White` and `Other` with `Black`.

7 How well does the model fit the data?

7.1 Pseudo-R² measures of fit

We will repeat the results for the model specified by

```
. use "lbw_working"
(Hosmer & Lemeshow data)
. logistic low i.smoke c.age c.lwt i.ht c.ftv i.race, baselevels vsquish
Logistic regression                                     Number of obs =    189
                                                        LR chi2(7)    =  26.82
                                                        Prob > chi2   = 0.0004
Log likelihood = -103.92653                             Pseudo R2     = 0.1143

------------------------------------------------------------------------------
         low | Odds ratio   Std. err.      z    P>|z|     [95% conf. interval]
-------------+----------------------------------------------------------------
       smoke |
   Nonsmoker |          1  (base)
      Smoker |   2.923724   1.142303     2.75   0.006     1.359473    6.287846
         age |   .9777151   .0347113    -0.63   0.526     .9119952    1.048171
         lwt |   .9827303   .0067607    -2.53   0.011     .9695685    .9960709
          ht |
          No |          1  (base)
         Yes |   5.740497    3.97489     2.52   0.012     1.477585    22.30215
         ftv |   1.037457   .1766005     0.22   0.829      .743147    1.448323
        race |
       White |          1  (base)
       Black |   3.463827   1.824364     2.36   0.018     1.233777     9.72469
       Other |   2.533944   1.087596     2.17   0.030     1.092578    5.876813
       _cons |   2.196049   2.541109     0.68   0.497     .2273492    21.21244
------------------------------------------------------------------------------
Note: _cons estimates baseline odds.
```

One way to evaluate model fit is by the pseudo-R^2. Does the relatively low pseudo-R^2 of 0.114, $p < 0.001$ mean that our model is not all that useful? Not necessarily. Despite the pseudo-R^2 being far less than 1, this model has much to like; we have predictors that substantially affect the odds of a low-birthweight newborn.

What is a pseudo-R^2, anyway? To answer this question and consider alternative measures of fit, we must install a package of community-contributed commands called `spost13` (Long and Freese 2014).[1] To download and install `spost13`, we will start by running the following command in the Command window:

```
. search spost13
```

1. This package is unavailable in the Statistical Software Components Archive.

This will bring up a Viewer window. We want to download and install the ado-files, which are in the package labeled

```
spost13_ado from https://spost.su.domains
    Distribution-date: 19Jul2020 / spost13_ado | SPost13 commands from Long
    and Freese (2014) / Regression Models for Categorical Outcomes using
    Stata, 3rd Edition. / Support www.indiana.edu/~jslsoc/spost.htm / Scott
    Long (jslong@indiana.edu) & Jeremy Freese (jfreese@stanford.edu)
```

Clicking on this link opens a second Viewer window listing many individual files. (The individual commands in the package have the filename extension of `.ado`.) An ado-file is like a do-file but is executed directly like a regular command. On the right side of the window, click on `click here to install`; all the commands will then be downloaded and installed on your computer.

Then run the `fitstat` postestimation command:

```
. fitstat

                           |   logistic
---------------------------+-------------
Log-likelihood             |
                     Model |   -103.927
            Intercept-only |   -117.336
---------------------------+-------------
Chi-square                 |
          Deviance(df=181) |    207.853
                  LR(df=7) |     26.819
                   p-value |      0.000
---------------------------+-------------
R2                         |
                  McFadden |      0.114
        McFadden(adjusted) |      0.046
              Cox-Snell/ML |      0.132
   Cragg-Uhler/Nagelkerke  |      0.186
                     Efron |      0.132
                  Tjur's D |      0.134
                     Count |      0.735
           Count(adjusted) |      0.153
---------------------------+-------------
IC                         |
                       AIC |    223.853
           AIC divided by N|      1.184
                 BIC(df=8) |    249.787
```

The list shows several pseudo-R^2 values that vary from 0.046 to 0.735. None of these values are the R^2 we get for a conventional ordinary least-squares (OLS) regression analysis, and they should *not* be interpreted as the proportion of variance explained. Among these measures of pseudo-R^2, we see that McFadden's (1974, 1987) R^2 is 0.114. This is the R^2 that Stata labels the pseudo-R^2. Maximum likelihood identifies the solution that maximizes a complex likelihood function. It is reasonable to compare different models using the size of the likelihood function. McFadden's R^2 compares the likelihood function of a solution with the likelihood function of a null (intercept-only) model:

$$R^2 = 1 - \frac{\text{log likelihood of full model}}{\text{log likelihood of intercept-only model}}$$

The `fitstat` command reports the log likelihood for the null model with no independent variables. This is labeled the `Intercept-only` model. The `fitstat` command reports that the likelihood for this null model is -117.336. We can get this by running an interception-only model ourselves:

```
. logistic low
Logistic regression                                     Number of obs =       189
                                                        LR chi2(0)    =     -0.00
                                                        Prob > chi2   =         .
Log likelihood = -117.336                               Pseudo R2     = -0.0000

------------------------------------------------------------------------------
         low |      Odds   Std. err.      z    P>|z|     [95% conf. interval]
-------------+----------------------------------------------------------------
       _cons |  .4538462   .0712429    -5.03   0.000     .3336495    .6173435
------------------------------------------------------------------------------
```

The log likelihood is -117.336 for the intercept-only model. By contrast, when we have the entire model, the log likelihood is -103.927. Both log likelihoods have negative values. Notably, the log likelihood for our model of -103.927 is larger (less negative) than the log likelihood of -117.336 when we include no predictors. The larger the likelihood, the better, so why not have a measure that compares the two values?

Hence, we use McFadden's R^2:

$$\text{McFadden's } R^2 = 1 - \frac{-103.927}{-117.336} = 0.114$$

McFadden's R^2 is the proportional increase in the log likelihood of our model compared with a model that has no predictors at all. This means that the full model has a log likelihood that is 11.4% larger than the model with no predictors. With conventional OLS regression, R^2 measures explained variance. Logistic regression does not explain variance. You may have read articles where experienced researchers misinterpret pseudo-R^2 as a measure of explained variance, but this is 100% wrong.

Some software reports the Cox–Snell R^2 (1989), which is labeled `Cox-Snell/ML` by `fitstat`. Here the Cox–Snell R^2 is 0.132. A limitation of the Cox–Snell R^2 is that its upper limit is not 1.0. It can be adjusted by its upper limit, Cox–Snell R^2/maximum value. The `fitstat` command reports the adjusted Cox–Snell R^2 of 0.186 under the label `Cragg-Uhler/Nagelkerke`, based on the adjustment from Cragg and Uhler (1970) and Nagelkerke (1991).

There is an excellent article by Paul Allison (2013) that compares McFadden's R^2 with the Cox–Snell R^2. He concludes as follows:

> "For years, I've been recommending the Cox and Snell R^2 over the McFadden R^2, but I've recently concluded that that was a mistake. I now believe that McFadden's R^2 is a better choice (Allison 2013)."

Allison discussed the third measure of R^2 as Tjur's R^2 (Tjur 2009). The `fitstat` command reports the absolute value as Tjur's $D = 0.134$. It has a more intuitive interpretation than either McFadden's R^2 or the Cox–Snell R^2.

To understand Tjur's R^2, we now use the `predict` command to predict the probability of each mother in our sample having a low-birthweight newborn:

```
. predict yhat if e(sample)
(option pr assumed; Pr(low))
```

We include the `if e(sample)` restriction, which is needed only when there are missing values. The individual probabilities of low birthweight generated from `predict` range from a low of 0.029 to a high of 0.788.

One way to assess how well our model fits the data is based on the `yhat` variable that we just predicted for each case. There are 130 newborns with a normal birthweight and 59 with a low birthweight. If our model is valid, it should predict a relatively high probability of low birthweight for the 59 newborns with a low birthweight. By contrast, our model should predict a low probability of low birthweight for newborns who had a normal birthweight.

We can get the mean predicted probability for mothers with low-birthweight newborns versus those without by using the `ttest` command:

```
. ttest yhat, by(low)
Two-sample t test with equal variances

   Group |     Obs        Mean    Std. err.   Std. dev.   [95% conf. interval]
---------+--------------------------------------------------------------------
      No |     130    .2703758    .0133461    .1521686    .2439703    .2967813
     Yes |      59    .4042567    .0228347    .1753964    .3585482    .4499653
---------+--------------------------------------------------------------------
Combined |     189    .3121693      .01244    .1710222    .2876293    .3367093
---------+--------------------------------------------------------------------
    diff |           -.1338809    .0250745               -.1833462   -.0844156
------------------------------------------------------------------------------
    diff = mean(No) - mean(Yes)                                   t =  -5.3393
H0: diff = 0                                     Degrees of freedom =      187

    Ha: diff < 0                 Ha: diff != 0                 Ha: diff > 0
 Pr(T < t) = 0.0000         Pr(|T| > |t|) = 0.0000          Pr(T > t) = 1.0000
```

The 59 mothers with low-birthweight newborns have a mean predicted probability of having a low-birthweight newborn of 0.404. A better model would have a much higher mean predicted probability. The 130 mothers with normal-birthweight newborns had a mean predicted probability of having a low-birthweight newborn of 0.270. These data show that we do a better job predicting the probability of normal-birthweight newborns. Tjur's D is just the absolute difference. Tjur's $|D| = |0.404 - 0.270| = 0.134$. (The `ttest` command is a convenient way to obtain the mean predicted probabilities and the difference, but the other results such as the p-values are not for Tjur's D; also see Paul Allison's discussion at https://statisticalhorizons.com/r2logistic/.)

Many researchers do not report any pseudo-R^2 values. This is often a justifiable omission:

1. None of these measures explain variance and should always be distinct from the R^2 used for OLS estimation models. If we had used OLS regression on the same model, ignoring the limitations discussed in chapter 5, the R^2 would have been 0.130. Generally, the pseudo-R^2 Stata reports is slightly lower than the R^2 if you incorrectly applied OLS regression.
2. Even when the pseudo-R^2 values are small, the independent variables may have strong, practically significant effects.

Our findings support the last point. Dramatic effects of variables such as smoking and hypertension contradict the low pseudo-R^2. If you need to report a goodness-of-fit measure, I recommend reporting Tjur's D using the `predict` and `ttest` commands or using Long and Freese's (2014) `fitstat` command.

7.2 Information criteria

Another way to evaluate model fit is to compare potential models and use information criteria to determine which model fits best. When adding predictors to a model, the log-likelihood function is expected to increase (become less negative) by chance. When comparing the fits of two models, some adjustment is needed when one of the models has more predictors. By chance, complex models with many variables will have a larger log likelihood. The Akaike information criterion (AIC) and Bayesian information criterion (BIC) allow you to compare the fits of two models by adding a penalty term reflecting the number of predictors in each model. This is done to offset the increased log likelihood due to chance. The AIC and BIC can also be used to compare models for the same dataset, even when they have different sets of predictors.

The AIC and BIC are closely related, with the BIC having a larger penalty term to offset increased model complexity. These are measures of goodness of fit and not tests. (In chapter 14, we will test for differences in nested models in which two models start with the same set of predictors and the second model adds additional predictors or interaction terms.) Typically, we do not interpret individual AIC or BIC values. Instead, we compare how two AICs or BICs differ across models that use the same sample. AICs and BICs are particularly useful when comparing models that are not nested as long as both models have the same outcome variable and are based on the same sample. For example, you might compare a model that has only demographic predictors with one that has only social network predictors.

The `fitstat` command reports three information criteria: AIC, AIC/N, and BIC. Note that there are different ways to calculate these measures in the literature; how this is done should be clear to readers.

We focus on the BIC to compare models. Whichever model has the smaller BIC has the better fit.

Long and Freese (2014) report a criterion for evaluating the difference between two models using the BIC. Remember that when you say a difference is weak, positive, strong, or very strong, the model with the smaller BIC is the model of choice.

Table 7.1. Guide to comparing the fits of two models

Strength of the difference	BIC
Weak	less than 2
Positive	2 to 6
Strong	6 to 10
Very strong	10 or more

7.3 Identifying cases that the model fits poorly

We can also examine how well our model fits in terms of predictions. Stata has several ways to identify individual observations that your model could do a better job of predicting. A straightforward way is to estimate the standardized residual for each observation. Below, we do this and evaluate the observations with large standardized residuals using a cutpoint of ±1.96 (corresponding to large z scores). After the logistic model is fit, we run the postestimation command `predict`. The `rstandard` option calculates the standardized residual.

```
. predict z, rstandard
. list id z if z > 1.96 | z < -1.96

     +---------------+
     | id          z |
     |---------------|
 13. | 98  -2.030126 |
132. | 10   2.826679 |
136. | 16   2.151387 |
147. | 28   2.591371 |
148. | 29   2.020887 |
     |---------------|
152. | 33   1.996653 |
155. | 36   2.968739 |
158. | 42   2.218422 |
170. | 57   2.123166 |
177. | 67   2.218422 |
     |---------------|
183. | 77   2.816813 |
     +---------------+
```

Eleven of the observations have large standardized residuals. With standardized residuals, we expect to have 5% of observations outside ±1.96, so these are not necessarily problematic. However, cases with large standardized residuals could be examined. These cases are people who have a coded value of 0 but were predicted to have a code of 1 or people who have a coded value of 1 but were predicted to have a code of 0. Perhaps there was a coding error. Would adding the additional predictors eliminate some of the outliers? This could give you ideas for a new model.

8 Sensitivity and specificity

8.1 Criteria for evaluating an analysis

No real-life model will perfectly predict an outcome such as which newborns will have a low birthweight, who will vote for the Democratic candidate in a US election, who has type 2 diabetes, who passes a driving test, or which children are ready for kindergarten. I will now introduce four criteria for evaluating predictions. These criteria are designed to develop a definitive screening test and are potentially helpful in prediction models. Analyzing sensitivity and specificity with a prediction model will likely dampen any overenthusiasm about the model.

To explore statistics for evaluating predictions, we will consider the "quick COVID" tests developed during the COVID-19 pandemic. These tests were self-administered and measured someone's level of antibodies. But how good were they?

We will use table 8.1 to clarify the four possible results. The columns show whether a person has COVID-19, and the rows show whether the person was predicted or classified as having COVID-19 based on the quick test.

Table 8.1. Sensitivity and specificity

Test result	Actual COVID-19 condition	
	Have COVID-19	Do not have COVID-19
Test detected positive COVID-19 classification	TP	FP
Test detected negative COVID-19 classification	FN Big problem	TN
Total	Total TP + FN	Total FP + TN

From this table, we will consider four criteria for evaluating the test.

False negatives (FNs): These were a massive problem with the quick tests. Many people tested negative but either had or were starting to develop COVID-19. This could happen because the test was inaccurate or because of a mistake in how the test was administered. The more likely explanation is that COVID-19 was in its early stages, which meant that the person did not meet the threshold of antibodies at the time of the test. But the quick test would still be negative, so people would be sent happily on their way. A day later, or even by the time they got home, they would be spreading COVID-19.

False positives (FPs): An FP occurs when someone does not have COVID-19 but receives a positive test result anyway. This would be a pain in the neck for individuals misadvised to self-isolate or for anyone who depended on physically being with those individuals. Fortunately, the tests had few FPs. This was a strength of the test; few people received a positive test result unless they truly had COVID-19.

Sensitivity: Sensitivity is how well the test finds the cases that have the outcome being tested for. Both the people in the cell marked true positive (TP) and those in the cell marked FN had COVID-19. Sensitivity is calculated as

$$\text{Sensitivity} = \frac{\text{TP}}{\text{TP} + \text{FN}}$$

Thus, in this case, sensitivity is the proportion of people who had COVID-19 and tested positive. The sensitivity of the quick test could have been better. Unfortunately, it produced many FNs, driving down the sensitivity.

Some people had COVID-19 but were asymptomatic. For them, the sensitivity was poor. This was a monumental problem because these people could still expose others to COVID-19. Many studies estimated the sensitivity both for people who had active symptoms and for people who had COVID-19 but were asymptomatic. Jegerlehner et al. (2001) reported that for those who showed symptoms, the sensitivity was 65.3%, but for those who were asymptomatic but had COVID-19, the sensitivity was just 44.0%. These sensitivity levels mean that many people mistakenly believed that they did not have COVID-19 based on the quick test. The quick test had 56.0% FNs among those who were asymptomatic and 34.7% FNs even among those who were symptomatic.

Specificity: Specificity refers to how well the test identifies people who do not have the outcome being tested for. In table 8.1, both the true negatives (TNs) and the FPs did not have COVID-19. Specificity is calculated as

$$\text{Specificity} = \frac{\text{TN}}{\text{TN} + \text{FP}}$$

The quick test had good specificity. There was only a 5.0% chance of an FP, and the specificity was 95.0% (Wölfl-Duchek et al. 2022), so you could be confident if your results indicated that you did not have COVID-19.

8.2 Estimation of sensitivity and specificity

Stata commands make it simple to calculate both sensitivity and specificity based on predictions from a logistic regression. Let us illustrate this by returning to the data on newborns' birthweights from previous chapters. First, we will rerun our logistic regression model:

```
. use "lbw_working"
(Hosmer & Lemeshow data)
. logistic low i.smoke age c.lwt i.ht c.ftv i.race, baselevels vsquish
  (output omitted)
```

Next we run the postestimation command `estat classification`, which, by default, assumes that any case that has predicted probability $\Pr \geq 0.50$ of being coded as 1 will be classified as positive. Thus, $\Pr \geq 0.50$ provides the default threshold for predicting a positive outcome. In our model, a positive outcome is a low-birthweight newborn. You can modify this default by specifying the value of $(1 - \Pr)$ in the `cutoff()` option.[1]

```
. estat classification
Logistic model for low

              ──────── True ────────
Classified |         D            ~D  |      Total
───────────┼──────────────────────────┼───────────
     +     |        16             7  |         23
     -     |        43           123  |        166
───────────┼──────────────────────────┼───────────
   Total   |        59           130  |        189
Classified + if predicted Pr(D) >= .5
True D defined as low != 0
──────────────────────────────────────────────────
Sensitivity                     Pr( +| D)   27.12%
Specificity                     Pr( -|~D)   94.62%
Positive predictive value       Pr( D| +)   69.57%
Negative predictive value       Pr(~D| -)   74.10%
──────────────────────────────────────────────────
False + rate for true ~D        Pr( +|~D)    5.38%
False - rate for true D         Pr( -| D)   72.88%
False + rate for classified +   Pr(~D| +)   30.43%
False - rate for classified -   Pr( D| -)   25.90%
──────────────────────────────────────────────────
Correctly classified                        73.54%
──────────────────────────────────────────────────
```

`D` means that the newborn has a low birthweight, coded as 1.
`~D` means that the newborn has a normal birthweight, coded as 0.
`+` means that the model predicts a low-birthweight newborn.
`-` means that the model predicts a normal-birthweight newborn.

1. This table shows that we had few (7) FPs—just 5.38% (7/130) of all normal-birthweight newborns. Very few of these mothers (`~D`, coded as 0) were predicted to have a low-birthweight newborn (`Classified +`).

1. Run `help r estat classification` for details on the `estat classification` command.

2. We had many (43) FNs—72.88% (43/59) of low-birthweight newborns. Most of the 59 mothers with a low-birthweight newborn (`D`, coded as 1) were predicted to have a normal-birthweight newborn (`Classified -`).

3. The sensitivity of our model would be terrible if we considered it a screening test. Only 27.12% (16/59) of the 59 mothers with a low-birthweight newborn, were "caught" based on our predictors. Our model provides valuable guidelines for expecting mothers—do not smoke and control your hypertension. However, we cannot use our model as a test to guide doctors when they need to plan for a low birthweight.

4. The specificity of our model, 94.62% (123/130) is excellent. Our model predicts which mothers will have a normal-birthweight newborn (`~D`) very well. We can tell an expecting mother that if she follows the guidelines based on the model—she should not smoke, and she should control her hypertension—she can be confident that she will have a normal-birthweight newborn.

What conclusions can we draw from the poor sensitivity and excellent specificity? Our specificity of 94.62% shows that we can predict which newborns will have a normal birthweight. Our sensitivity of 27.12% shows that we cannot confidently predict which newborns will have a clinically low birthweight (`D`). We must recognize that our model predicts a high percentage (72.88%) of FNs.

Most researchers do not check the sensitivity and specificity of logistic models. The sensitivity and specificity are needed when developing a screening test. They can also help researchers understand the practical significance of their model, and they allow a more in-depth analysis of the practical effectiveness of the model.

9 Receiver operating characteristic curves and cutpoints for screening tests

Logistic regression is widely used for developing screening tests. A person's score on one of these tests is used to decide whether the person passes it. Some examples are the tests people take to qualify for a driver's license, gain admittance to a university, or obtain financial assistance. Screening tests based on logistic regression models are widely used in medicine and epidemiology. In chapter 8, we saw how sensitivity and specificity can be used to evaluate the practical significance of a test. In this chapter, we take this further.

First, we introduce receiver operating characteristic (ROC) curves and then explore ways to find the optimal cutpoint (score) on a quantitative test to decide who passes and who fails. ROC curves have been used in radar systems for the last century. Radar operators needed to find the optimal signal threshold to distinguish such things as the type of airplane that was approaching. For example, they needed to know whether the aircraft posed a threat or was a friendly passenger plane.

A ROC curve finds the cutpoint that balances the rate of true positives (sensitivity) against the rate of true negatives (specificity).

We want to decide on the optimum score on a test that classifies who should be in or out of the category. We need three things:

1. **The test itself.** This might be one of the following:

    a. A depression score calculated using the number of items about symptoms of depression that you check as they apply to you.

    b. An antigen test for COVID-19 using the level of an antibody in a sample of your blood.

    c. A kindergarten readiness test using the number of correct answers to questions.

    d. A test for dementia that uses the number of correct answers to questions.

2. **A group of "known" people to have the measured outcome.** These people serve as the criteria for defining the cutpoint for our new test. Suppose that we have a test to see who needs medical intervention because of depression. The known group might be people who highly skilled psychiatrists have previously evaluated.

3. **A sample of people we want to classify as belonging or not belonging to the group or category.** We need to find the cutpoint on the test that best classifies who belongs in or out. This involves finding the optimum test score to balance sensitivity and specificity.

9.1 ROC curves

Suppose that we want a screening test to decide which high school students belong in the academic program. If we make the cutpoint too low, we sacrifice specificity for sensitivity. If we make the cutpoint too high, we sacrifice sensitivity for specificity. A low cutpoint will place students in the academic program who will gain little and find the challenge overwhelming (false positive). However, with a high cutpoint, we will exclude students from the academic program who would have gained a lot and found the challenge enriching (false negative).

To illustrate how to find the optimal cutpoint, we will elaborate on an example from UCLA's Institute for Digital Research in Education. Open their data now:

```
. use https://stats.idre.ucla.edu/stat/stata/notes/hsb2
(highschool and beyond (200 cases))
```

This dataset contains data on 200 teenagers selected from the High School and Beyond study. We aim to decide which students belong in the academic program and which do not. First, we need a criterion group of students known to benefit from the academic program. We will use the students already in the academic program. This is not a great choice, but it is our only choice for this dataset. It would be much better if we restricted our criterion group to students who have done well in the academic program and feel they have benefited from this placement. You can see how selecting your criterion group is tricky, and often, the choice is far from ideal. If you are developing a screening test, you must focus on finding a highly qualified criterion group.

To develop a cutpoint, we need a test. We will use a standardized math test. Its mean is 52.645, its standard deviation is 9.368, and its range is 33 to 75.

The outcome variable is a binary criterion variable (students who should belong in the academic program versus those who should not). We are dubiously assuming that all the students in our test sample who are already in the academic program belong there. The dataset has a variable, `prog`, coded as 1 for `general`, 2 for `academic`, and 3 for `vocation`. We can use the `fre` command to view the data.

```
. fre prog
prog — type of program
```

		Freq.	Percent	Valid	Cum.
Valid	1 general	45	22.50	22.50	22.50
	2 academic	105	52.50	52.50	75.00
	3 vocation	50	25.00	25.00	100.00
	Total	200	100.00	100.00	

We will generate a new variable, `academic`, coded as 0 for `Not academic` and 1 for `Academic`. We combine the `general` and `vocation` categories into the `Not academic` group.

```
. recode prog (1 = 0 "Not academic") (3 = 0 "Not academic")  ///
> (2 = 1 "Academic"), generate(academic)
(200 differences between prog and academic)
```

We now see that 95 students are in the `Not academic` program and 105 are in the `Academic` program.

```
. fre academic
academic — RECODE of prog (type of program)
```

		Freq.	Percent	Valid	Cum.
Valid	0 Not academic	95	47.50	47.50	47.50
	1 Academic	105	52.50	52.50	100.00
	Total	200	100.00	100.00	

Let us look at the relationship between math test scores and whether the students with these scores are in the `Not academic` program or the `Academic` program:

```
. table math academic
```

	RECODE of prog (type of program)		
	Not academic	Academic	Total
math score			
33	1		1
35	1		1
37	1		1
38	1	1	2
39	6		6
40	10		10
41	5	2	7
42	6	1	7
43	3	4	7
44	3	1	4
45	4	4	8
46	7	1	8
47	3		3
48	1	4	5
49	4	6	10
50	2	5	7
51	3	5	8
52	4	2	6
53	2	5	7
54	4	6	10
55	3	2	5
56	5	2	7
57	6	7	13
58	3	3	6
59		2	2
60	2	3	5
61	2	5	7
62		4	4
63	1	4	5
64		5	5
65		3	3
66	1	3	4
67		2	2
68		1	1
69		2	2
70		1	1
71		4	4
72		3	3
73		1	1
75	1	1	2
Total	95	105	200

This table shows that more students with lower scores are in the `Not academic` program than in the `Academic` program. Most students with high scores are in the `Academic` program. Still, some students in the `Not academic` program score well on the test, while some students in the `Academic` program do not. Notice that one student in the `Not academic` program was tied for the highest score on the math test.

To get the optimal cutpoint, we use the ROC curve. Stata generates this curve using the `roctab` command, which here plots the math score's sensitivity versus 1 − specificity. The `detail`, `graph`, and `summary` options give us information about the curve. `detail` produces a table showing the sensitivity and specificity for every observed score on the math test. As expected, the table shows how greater sensitivity means worse specificity. Unless you have a good reason to emphasize sensitivity or specificity, the best cutpoint is a score on math that balances sensitivity and specificity.

```
. roctab academic math, detail graph summary ///
> text(-.15 0 "Perfect specificity" -.15 .95 "Zero specificity")
Detailed report of sensitivity and specificity
------------------------------------------------------------------------------
                                          Correctly
Cutpoint      Sensitivity   Specificity   classified          LR+          LR-
------------------------------------------------------------------------------
( >= 33 )        100.00%         0.00%       52.50%        1.0000
( >= 35 )        100.00%         1.05%       53.00%        1.0106       0.0000
( >= 37 )        100.00%         2.11%       53.50%        1.0215       0.0000
( >= 38 )        100.00%         3.16%       54.00%        1.0326       0.0000
( >= 39 )         99.05%         4.21%       54.00%        1.0340       0.2262
( >= 40 )         99.05%        10.53%       57.00%        1.1070       0.0905
( >= 41 )         99.05%        21.05%       62.00%        1.2546       0.0452
( >= 42 )         97.14%        26.32%       63.50%        1.3184       0.1086
( >= 43 )         96.19%        32.63%       66.00%        1.4278       0.1167
( >= 44 )         92.38%        35.79%       65.50%        1.4387       0.2129
( >= 45 )         91.43%        38.95%       66.50%        1.4975       0.2201
( >= 46 )         87.62%        43.16%       66.50%        1.5414       0.2869
( >= 47 )         86.67%        50.53%       69.50%        1.7518       0.2639
( >= 48 )         86.67%        53.68%       71.00%        1.8712       0.2484
( >= 49 )         82.86%        54.74%       69.50%        1.8306       0.3132
( >= 50 )         77.14%        58.95%       68.50%        1.8791       0.3878
( >= 51 )         72.38%        61.05%       67.00%        1.8584       0.4524
( >= 52 )         67.62%        64.21%       66.00%        1.8894       0.5043
( >= 53 )         65.71%        68.42%       67.00%        2.0810       0.5011
( >= 54 )         60.95%        70.53%       65.50%        2.0680       0.5537
( >= 55 )         55.24%        74.74%       64.50%        2.1865       0.5989
( >= 56 )         53.33%        77.89%       65.00%        2.4127       0.5991
( >= 57 )         51.43%        83.16%       66.50%        3.0536       0.5841
( >= 58 )         44.76%        89.47%       66.00%        4.2524       0.6174
( >= 59 )         41.90%        92.63%       66.00%        5.6871       0.6272
( >= 60 )         40.00%        92.63%       65.00%        5.4286       0.6477
( >= 61 )         37.14%        94.74%       64.50%        7.0571       0.6635
( >= 62 )         32.38%        96.84%       63.00%       10.2540       0.6982
( >= 63 )         28.57%        96.84%       61.00%        9.0476       0.7376
( >= 64 )         24.76%        97.89%       59.50%       11.7619       0.7686
( >= 65 )         20.00%        97.89%       57.00%        9.5000       0.8172
( >= 66 )         17.14%        97.89%       55.50%        8.1429       0.8464
( >= 67 )         14.29%        98.95%       54.50%       13.5715       0.8663
( >= 68 )         12.38%        98.95%       53.50%       11.7620       0.8855
( >= 69 )         11.43%        98.95%       53.00%       10.8572       0.8951
( >= 70 )          9.52%        98.95%       52.00%        9.0477       0.9144
( >= 71 )          8.57%        98.95%       51.50%        8.1429       0.9240
( >= 72 )          4.76%        98.95%       49.50%        4.5238       0.9625
( >= 73 )          1.90%        98.95%       48.00%        1.8095       0.9914
( >= 75 )          0.95%        98.95%       47.50%        0.9048       1.0010
( >  75 )          0.00%       100.00%       47.50%                     1.0000
------------------------------------------------------------------------------
```

Obs	ROC area	Std. err.	Asymptotic normal [95% conf.	interval]
200	0.7647	0.0330	0.70002	0.82931

Notice that using the lowest score on the test, 33, as the cutpoint produces 100% sensitivity simply because it classifies everybody as being in the `Academic` criterion group. However, a cutpoint of 33 does this by also classifying students who do not "belong" in the program as `Academic`. Hence, the specificity for a score of 33 is 0%.

The `graph` option produces the graph in figure 9.1. Because sensitivity and specificity are inversely related, the graph plots sensitivity versus 1−specificity. Using 1−specificity on the horizontal axis reverses the specificity score. This means that a score of 0 on the horizontal axis represents 100% specificity, and a score of 1.0 represents 0% specificity. A perfect cutpoint would have coordinates of $(0, 1)$, which would put it in the upper-left corner (1.0 on sensitivity and 0.0 on 1−specificity). No number of correct answers on our test comes close to this ideal point! Below is the resulting graph. Note that I specified the `text()` option to add the labels `Perfect specificity` and `Zero specificity`.

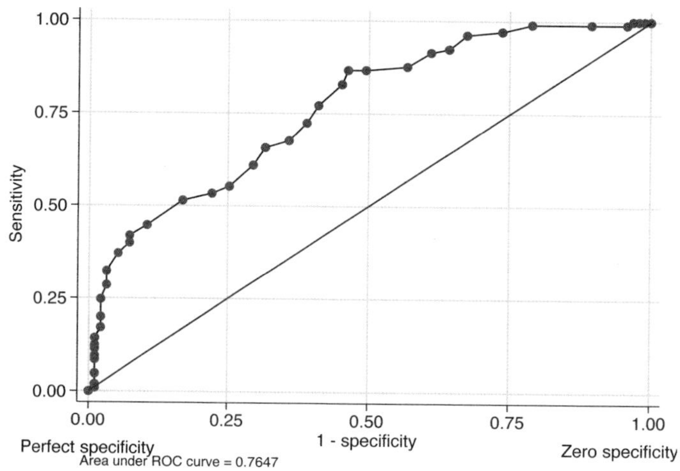

Figure 9.1. ROC curve

The 45-degree line is what we would expect if there was no connection between the math test and being in the academic program. The curved line shows that sensitivity improves rapidly as the specificity worsens very slightly initially. A test will have a curve well above the 45-degree line, and the size of the area of the graph between the curved line and the 45-degree line will be used to evaluate our test.

The summary option at the end of the roctab command reports the area under the ROC curve.

```
                      ROC                    Asymptotic normal
           Obs        area    Std. err.    [95% conf. interval]
         ------------------------------------------------------------
           200      0.7647       0.0330       0.70002     0.82931
```

The guideline for a good value of the area under the curve varies by field of study. One standard is that a ROC between 0.7 to 0.8 is "acceptable", 0.8 to 0.9 is "good", and over 0.9 is "excellent". Thus, using the math score to place students in the academic program is acceptable. However, it is neither an excellent nor a good standard. All the scores on the math test to select the students who get in the academic program will exclude students who would benefit from the program (false negative). Similarly, all scores will include several students who do not belong in the academic program (false positive).

So what is the best cutpoint? Given the ROC table, what score would you pick as the cutpoint that best balances sensitivity and specificity? You might pick a score of 48. This cutpoint has a sensitivity of 86.7%, a specificity of 53.7%, and 71.0% of the cases will be in the "right" category. Just from inspecting the ROC table, a score of 48 seems to be a reasonable cutpoint.

Can we have a more formalized way to select the optimal cutpoint? Clayton (2013) from the ANZDATA registry in Australia created a community-contributed command, cutpt (run ssc install cutpt to install it). His command finds the cutpoint that optimizes sensitivity and specificity. cutpt provides three ways of identifying the optimal cutpoint:

1. The Liu method picks the value that maximizes the product of (sensitivity $\times$ specificity).
2. The Youden method maximizes the sum of sensitivity and specificity.
3. The nearest to $(0, 1)$ method finds the cutpoint on the ROC curve closest to $(0, 1)$ because that point would have perfect sensitivity and specificity.

```
. cutpt academic math
Empirical cutpoint estimation
Method:                                  Liu
Reference variable:                      academic (0=neg, 1=pos)
Classification variable:                 math
Empirical optimal cutpoint:              47.5
Sensitivity at cutpoint:                 0.87
Specificity at cutpoint:                 0.54
Area under ROC curve at cutpoint:        0.70
```

The Liu method is the default. You could add the youden or nearest option to use one of the other methods. Using the default method, we find that the optimal cutpoint is a score of 47.5 on the math test. It has 87% sensitivity and 54% specificity.

This means that it will catch 87% of the people who "should" be in the academic program and miss only 100% − 87% = 13% of them. It is essential to recognize a significant limitation of the readiness test for the academic program: using a cutpoint of 47.5 would exclude 13% of the qualified students who would benefit from the academic program. This would be a significant setback to a person with the potential to pursue an advanced academic career. By contrast, several students who are unprepared for the academic program would be misplaced. A ROC analysis shows the limitations of this test. It would be helpful to report the sensitivity and specificity for a given cutpoint for any test used for placement or diagnosis. We should be wary of relying on a single objective test without high sensitivity and specificity.

The `cutpt` command reports that the area under the ROC curve at cutpoint is 0.70. This should not be confused with the more widely used area under the ROC curve, which is 0.765 from the `roctab` command.

9.2 Comparing tests

Is the math test the best to decide who to include in the academic program? What about a general intelligence test, a science test, or a social science test? Stata's `roccomp` command can help us determine which is best by comparing pairs of tests. Let us compare the math test with the science test:

```
. roccomp academic math science, graph summary
                              ROC                    Asymptotic normal
                  Obs        area     Std. err.    [95% conf. interval]
--------------------------------------------------------------------------
math              200      0.7647       0.0330      0.70002     0.82931
science           200      0.6260       0.0397      0.54811     0.70392
--------------------------------------------------------------------------
H0: area(math) = area(science)
    chi2(1) =     18.97       Prob>chi2 =    0.0000
```

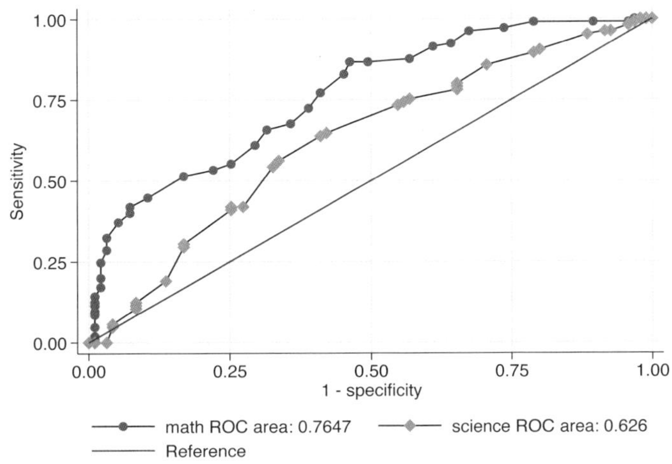

Figure 9.2. ROC curves comparing math test with science test

Figure 9.2 shows more area under the ROC curve for the math test (0.7647) than for the science test (just 0.626). Indeed, the area under the ROC curve for the science test falls below the minimum standard of 0.70 for an acceptable test.

What is the p-value for the difference in area between math and science tests? The `roccomp` command reports a $\chi^2(1) = 18.97$, $p < 0.001$, which indicates that the areas are not equivalent for the two tests.

10 Predictions using the margins command

10.1 What is better than reporting coefficients and odds ratios?

Odds ratios (ORs) are a big improvement over just reporting the logistic regression coefficients (Bs), but they can be misleading. ORs often need clarification when the goal is measuring the risk or the difference in the risk rather than the ratio of two odds. An alternative to the OR is the relative risk (see section 15.4). ORs will show a stronger effect than the relative risk (see section 15.4). The OR will be further above 1.0 when the relative risk is greater than 1.0. The OR will be further below 1.0 when the relative risk is less than 1.0. In other words, the OR should not be interpreted as the relative risk because it will exaggerate the relative risk for the outcome.

When predicting a rare outcome, the OR can be highly misleading. For example, doubling the odds of a rare event may still leave us with a rare event. What is your risk of having a fatal accident driving to a neighborhood grocery store today? A light rain may double the odds, but this tells us little about the actual risk. The risk of a fatal accident in a single ride to a neighborhood grocery store remains infinitesimally tiny. We are often more interested in what the light rain means for the actual risk (probability) of a fatal accident than what the light rain means for the odds. If the actual risk difference is trivial, then that should be our focus.

The `margins` command allows us to move beyond simply reporting Bs and ORs. `margins` provides an accurate picture of how variation across the predictors influences the probability of the outcome. This is precisely what we want to know. Determining what effect a mother's smoking has on the probability of having a low-birthweight newborn, controlling for other covariates, is far more informative than reporting just the B and OR. We will illustrate how to use `margins` using data on an adult's risk of having high blood pressure. You could repeat these steps using the birthweight data as an exercise.

10.2 Data preparation

We will use `nhanes2l.dta` to predict who has high blood pressure. These are data from the *Second National Health and Nutrition Examination Survey* and have 10,351 observations (McDowell et al. 1981). A subset of this dataset can be downloaded directly from Stata because it is used in Stata's documentation. We want to predict how likely people are to have high blood pressure depending on their age, body mass index (BMI), and sex. `nhanes21.dta` uses a single `Male` or `Female` item to measure sex, like many other datasets. Although this does not let us consider the potentially complex relationships between the LBGTQ+ community and high blood pressure, it will suffice for our learning exercise.

We begin this with the expectation that your risk of high blood pressure is greater if you are older, have a higher BMI, and are male. Open `nhanes21.dta` using

```
. webuse nhanes21
(Second National Health and Nutrition Examination Survey)
```

First, we summarize these variables:

```
. summarize highbp age bmi sex
```

Variable	Obs	Mean	Std. dev.	Min	Max
highbp	10,351	.4227611	.494022	0	1
age	10,351	47.57965	17.21483	20	74
bmi	10,351	25.5376	4.914969	12.3856	61.1297
sex	10,351	1.525167	.4993904	1	2

Both `age` and `bmi` are quantitative variables; `highbp` and `sex` are categorical. Let us run the `fre` command for our categorical variables:

```
. fre highbp sex
```

highbp — High blood pressure

		Freq.	Percent	Valid	Cum.
Valid	0	5975	57.72	57.72	57.72
	1	4376	42.28	42.28	100.00
	Total	10351	100.00	100.00	

sex — Sex

		Freq.	Percent	Valid	Cum.
Valid	1 Male	4915	47.48	47.48	47.48
	2 Female	5436	52.52	52.52	100.00
	Total	10351	100.00	100.00	

Notice that `highbp` lacks value labels. We will add them:

```
. label define hi 0 "No" 1 "Yes"
. label values highbp hi
```

The sex variable uses codes of 1 and 2. Although it is unnecessary, we can recode them to 0 and 1, generating a new variable, female:

```
. recode sex (1=0 "Male") (2=1 "Female"), generate(female)
(10,351 differences between sex and female)
```

Finally, we will check our work:

```
. fre highbp female
highbp — High blood pressure

                    Freq.   Percent    Valid      Cum.
Valid   0 No         5975     57.72    57.72     57.72
        1 Yes        4376     42.28    42.28    100.00
        Total       10351    100.00   100.00

female — RECODE of sex (Sex)

                    Freq.   Percent    Valid      Cum.
Valid   0 Male       4915     47.48    47.48     47.48
        1 Female     5436     52.52    52.52    100.00
        Total       10351    100.00   100.00
```

Because we have modified these variables, we save the data to our working directory using a name different from the original dataset's:

```
. save "nhanes21_working", replace
(file nhanes21_working.dta not found)
file nhanes21_working.dta saved
```

10.3 Estimating the ORs

We begin by running logistic regression to predict high blood pressure using age, bmi, and female:

```
. logistic highbp c.age c.bmi i.female, baselevels vsquish
Logistic regression                                    Number of obs =  10,351
                                                       LR chi2(3)    = 2410.54
                                                       Prob > chi2   =  0.0000
Log likelihood = -5845.4948                            Pseudo R2     =  0.1709

      highbp   Odds ratio   Std. err.      z    P>|z|     [95% conf. interval]

         age     1.047058   .0014632   32.91   0.000     1.044194     1.04993
         bmi     1.147006    .005827   27.00   0.000     1.135642    1.158484
      female
        Male            1  (base)
      Female     .6172715   .0278625  -10.69   0.000     .5650079    .6743695
       _cons     .0029059   .0004428  -38.33   0.000     .0021556    .0039174

Note: _cons estimates baseline odds.
```

This shows that women have much lower odds than men (OR $= 0.617$, $p < 0.001$) of having high blood pressure. Being older (OR $= 1.047$, $p < 0.001$) and having a higher BMI (OR $= 1.147$, $p < 0.001$) increase the odds of having high blood pressure.

10.4 The margins command

We will now estimate the risk. There are two ways to do so. First, we can predict the probability of high blood pressure for all 10,351 people. The `predict` command produces predicted probabilities by default. After running logistic regression, we run

```
. predict prob
(option pr assumed; Pr(highbp))
```

Second, we can use the `margins` postestimation command, which has much more general utility than the `predict` command. For logistic regression, `margins` estimates the probability of the outcome. It also supplies the data needed for generating graphs of the relationships between predictors of interest and predicted probabilities using `marginsplot` (see chapter 11). `margins` is one of the most powerful commands in Stata. We will touch only on a few of its applications here. Note that different fields of study and other statistical software use the term "margin" differently. This book follows Stata's use of the term.[1]

10.4.1 Estimating risk for categorical predictors

Suppose that we wanted to see if there is a difference in the risk of high blood pressure between women and men. If we did not control for other covariates, we could create a 2×2 table:

```
. table highbp female, statistic(percent, across (highbp))
```

	RECODE of sex (Sex)		
	Male	Female	Total
High blood pressure			
No	53.12	61.88	57.72
Yes	46.88	38.12	42.28
Total	100.00	100.00	100.00

This table shows that 46.88% of men have been diagnosed with high blood pressure compared with 38.12% of women. We also could have used `tabulate` with the `chi2` option to provide a χ^2 test and p-value for the association between sex and high blood pressure.

1. [R] **margins** defines margins as "statistics calculated from predictions of a previously fit model at fixed values of some covariates and averaging or otherwise integrating over the remaining covariates".

This straightforward solution assumes that we do not need to control for covariates. In a large study, you would likely control for risky behavior like smoking, race, social capital (education and income), and health risks (BMI and age). The **margins** command after logistic regression lets us do this.

We will illustrate the effect of **female** on the risk of high blood pressure. For simplicity, we will keep just two control variables: **bmi** and **age**. First, we will run the logistic regression:

```
. logistic highbp c.age c.bmi i.female, baselevels vsquish
  (output omitted)
```

The **i.** is necessary for categorical variables in the **logistic** command. However, it is not needed in the **margins** command, because **margins** requires that the variables specified immediately after the command be categorical variables from **logistic**. Even so, I routinely include **i.** in **margins** as a reminder when scanning over a do-file. The command name, **margins**, is followed by the categorical predictor:

```
. margins i.female

Predictive margins                              Number of obs = 10,351
Model VCE: OIM

Expression: Pr(highbp), predict()
```

	Margin	Delta-method std. err.	z	P>|z|	[95% conf.	interval]
female						
Male	.4699816	.0062053	75.74	0.000	.4578195	.4821436
Female	.3771019	.0059595	63.28	0.000	.3654215	.3887823

The column labeled **Margin** provides the estimated probability of the outcome adjusting for the covariates. Specifically, it computes the average predicted probability as if everyone were male but with age and BMI as they are observed in the data. Then it does the same thing but as if everyone were female. The difference in risk across sexes has changed very little compared with when we had no control variables. Adjusting for BMI and age, the expected risk of women having high blood pressure is $\Pr_{\text{female}} = 0.377$ (compared with $\Pr_{\text{female}} = 0.381$ without controls). The expected risk for men is $\Pr_{\text{male}} = 0.470$ (compared with $\Pr_{\text{male}} = 0.469$ without controls).

The table also reports z tests, which are irrelevant here. They test whether the probability is different from 0.0. Unless we hypothesize that the risk of high blood pressure is 0 for either women or men, the z score and p-value should be ignored. On the other hand, the 95% confidence intervals are much more helpful. A wide confidence interval might indicate that our sample was too small to have adequate power.

How can we statistically test whether the risk of high blood pressure for women is lower than for men? To find out, we will specify the `dydx()` option (change in y | change in x), which provides a test of the difference in risk. Importantly, unlike a simple difference-of-proportion test (`prtest highbp, by(female)`), `dydx()` tests for the difference controlling for age and BMI. It is a valuable option whenever you are testing the difference in a proportion but need to control for confounding variables.

```
. margins, dydx(i.female)

Average marginal effects                          Number of obs = 10,351
Model VCE: OIM

Expression: Pr(highbp), predict()
dy/dx wrt:  1.female

------------------------------------------------------------------------------
             |            Delta-method
             |      dy/dx   std. err.      z    P>|z|     [95% conf. interval]
-------------+----------------------------------------------------------------
      female |
     Female  |  -.0928796   .0086035   -10.80   0.000    -.1097421   -.0760172
------------------------------------------------------------------------------
Note: dy/dx for factor levels is the discrete change from the base level.
```

We conclude the following:

1. The expected risk of high blood pressure is 0.377 for women compared with 0.470 for men.

2. The 0.093 advantage for women has a p-value < 0.001.

This will be clearer to most readers than reporting the B, -0.482, or its OR, 0.617.

10.4.2 Estimating the risk for quantitative predictors

Unlike categorical variables, quantitative predictors have many potential values. The `age` variable ranges from 20 to 74, and `bmi` ranges from 12.386 to 61.130. One solution is to select a few specific values for quantitative variables and estimate expected risk at the chosen values. We will pick values that represent the range in the predictor, and we must choose wisely. We will specify the values we like with the `at()` option.

How does the risk of high blood pressure vary across lifespan? Below, we specify ages 20, 30, 40, 50, 60, and 70. Notice that when we used `margins` with a categorical variable, we listed the predictor before the comma. With a quantitative variable, we listed the predictor after the comma using the `at()` option:[2]

```
. margins, at(age = (20 30 40 50 60 70))
```

2. The last parenthesis matches up with the first parenthesis after the `at()`. I find the last parenthesis easy to forget when specifying this option.

A more economical way of specifying these age values is with the following command. The `at()` option specifies to start with `age` = 20 and increase by 10 years at a time, stopping at `age` = 70.

```
. margins, at(age=(20(10)70))

Predictive margins                                Number of obs = 10,351
Model VCE: OIM

Expression: Pr(highbp), predict()
1._at: age = 20
2._at: age = 30
3._at: age = 40
4._at: age = 50
5._at: age = 60
6._at: age = 70
```

	Margin	Delta-method std. err.	z	P>|z|	[95% conf.	interval]
_at						
1	.1789776	.0064844	27.60	0.000	.1662684	.1916868
2	.2488994	.0061534	40.45	0.000	.2368389	.2609599
3	.3342081	.0053493	62.48	0.000	.3237237	.3446926
4	.4315122	.0049557	87.07	0.000	.4217992	.4412252
5	.5345363	.005916	90.35	0.000	.5229412	.5461314
6	.6353806	.0075453	84.21	0.000	.6205921	.6501691

These results show that the expected risk of high blood pressure increases from a probability of 0.179 for a 20-year-old (coded as 1) to a probability of 0.635 for a 70-year-old (coded as 6). This controls for BMI and sex. This result is far easier to understand and more revealing than reporting the OR for age as 1.047.

10.4.3 Estimating for a combination of categorical and quantitative variables

So far, we have accounted for BMI and sex by calculating the predicted probability for each observation using the observed values of BMI and sex and then averaging these predictions. Therefore, we are suggesting that the expected proportion of older individuals with high blood pressure is higher than that of younger individuals, assuming that these groups have the same distributions of BMI and sex as in the population. Alternatively, we could adjust for sex by estimating average predicted probabilities for females and males. Now we will estimate the risk for various combinations of BMI and sex.

```
. margins i.female, at(c.age=(20(10)70))
Predictive margins                                  Number of obs = 10,351
Model VCE: OIM

Expression: Pr(highbp), predict()
1._at: age = 20
2._at: age = 30
3._at: age = 40
4._at: age = 50
5._at: age = 60
6._at: age = 70
```

	Margin	Delta-method std. err.	z	P>|z|	[95% conf.	interval]
_at#female						
1#Male	.2126897	.0078847	26.97	0.000	.197236	.2281435
1#Female	.1479694	.00637	23.23	0.000	.1354845	.1604543
2#Male	.2910523	.0077518	37.55	0.000	.2758592	.3062455
2#Female	.2092569	.0066701	31.37	0.000	.1961837	.22233
3#Male	.3839854	.0073139	52.50	0.000	.3696504	.3983204
3#Female	.2868339	.0066632	43.05	0.000	.2737742	.2998935
4#Male	.48651	.0072373	67.22	0.000	.4723251	.5006949
4#Female	.3791402	.0068331	55.49	0.000	.3657476	.3925328
5#Male	.5909352	.0078871	74.92	0.000	.5754768	.6063935
5#Female	.4813567	.0077499	62.11	0.000	.4661672	.4965463
6#Male	.6887881	.0087079	79.10	0.000	.671721	.7058553
6#Female	.5858902	.0091873	63.77	0.000	.5678835	.6038969

These results give us the estimated probabilities for women and men at each age point, controlling for BMI. For example, the expected risk of high blood pressure for a 20-year-old man is 0.213 compared with 0.148 for a 20-year-old woman while controlling for BMI by setting it to its observed values. Notice that we have not allowed for an interaction between sex and age. The advantage women have may decrease or increase with age. This requires adding an interaction term, `female` × `age` (see chapter 13).

Suppose that we are interested in sex differences adjusting for fixed values of age and BMI. This can produce many combinations, so let us pick just a few. For age, we pick 20, 40, and 70 to represent young, middle-aged, and old, respectively. For BMI, we pick BMIs of 20, 30, and 50 to stand for a low BMI, a marginally obese BMI, and a morbidly obese BMI, respectively.

We put the categorical predictor `female` before the comma. After the comma, we specify our selected numeric values in the `at()` option. Pay special attention to the parentheses:

```
. margins i.female, at(age=(20 40 70) bmi=(20 30 50))
Adjusted predictions                                  Number of obs = 10,351
Model VCE: OIM

Expression: Pr(highbp), predict()
1._at: age = 20
       bmi = 20
2._at: age = 20
       bmi = 30
3._at: age = 20
       bmi = 50
4._at: age = 40
       bmi = 20
5._at: age = 40
       bmi = 30
6._at: age = 40
       bmi = 50
7._at: age = 70
       bmi = 20
8._at: age = 70
       bmi = 30
9._at: age = 70
       bmi = 50
```

	Margin	Delta-method std. err.	z	P>|z|	[95% conf.	interval]
_at#female						
1#Male	.1017241	.0054231	18.76	0.000	.091095	.1123533
1#Female	.0653351	.003873	16.87	0.000	.0577441	.072926
2#Male	.3086027	.0118329	26.08	0.000	.2854106	.3317948
2#Female	.2160041	.0097659	22.12	0.000	.1968634	.2351449
3#Male	.8739611	.0146413	59.69	0.000	.8452648	.9026575
3#Female	.8106132	.0202604	40.01	0.000	.7709035	.8503228
4#Male	.2212287	.0076703	28.84	0.000	.2061951	.2362622
4#Female	.1491902	.0060285	24.75	0.000	.1373745	.1610058
5#Male	.528228	.0101092	52.25	0.000	.5084143	.5480417
5#Female	.4086826	.0098729	41.39	0.000	.3893321	.428033
6#Male	.9456351	.0065952	143.38	0.000	.9327088	.9585614
6#Female	.914799	.009853	92.84	0.000	.8954874	.9341106
7#Male	.5302175	.0127032	41.74	0.000	.5053198	.5551152
7#Female	.4106137	.012184	33.70	0.000	.3867335	.4344939
8#Male	.8164637	.0073866	110.53	0.000	.8019863	.8309412
8#Female	.7330444	.0089963	81.48	0.000	.715412	.7506768
9#Male	.9857364	.0018638	528.87	0.000	.9820833	.9893894
9#Female	.977095	.002897	337.28	0.000	.9714169	.9827731

This produces 18 expected probabilities. In chapter 11, we will use the **marginsplot** command to graph results like these. A graph is a great way to represent what might otherwise be seen as an overwhelming list of risk values. Consider the last two rows of the table, **9#Male** and **9#Female**. They combine high age (70) and high BMI (50). At this level, men and women have about the same risk. Consider the people who are 40 years old with BMIs of 30, **5#Male** and **5#Female**. At this age, women have a lower risk: the expected probability of women having high blood pressure is 0.409 versus 0.528 for men.

You can also specify any combination of values for the predictors. What if you want to estimate the probability of high blood pressure for Bhavani and Ahmed? They are both 32.5 years old and have BMIs of 26.

```
. margins i.female, at(age=(32.5) bmi=(26))
Adjusted predictions                                    Number of obs = 10,351
Model VCE: OIM

Expression: Pr(highbp), predict()
At: age = 32.5
    bmi =   26

--------------------------------------------------------------------------------
             |            Delta-method
             |     Margin   std. err.      z    P>|z|     [95% conf. interval]
-------------+------------------------------------------------------------------
      female |
        Male |   .3142178   .0084302    37.27   0.000      .297695    .3307407
      Female |   .2204717   .0071669    30.76   0.000     .2064248    .2345185
--------------------------------------------------------------------------------
```

We see that Bhavani's probability is 0.220. Ahmed's probability is higher (0.314). Try this for your scores on these variables.

The **margins** command is one of the most powerful commands in Stata. There is extensive documentation in the *Stata Base Reference Manual* ([R] **margins**). A good source is Williams' (2012) highly accessible introductory article, written when **margins** was relatively new. A more recent article is Uberti (2022), which goes into more detail and features. There are several ways to adjust for the covariates in a model that we have not discussed.

11 Graphic presentation using the marginsplot command

11.1 When and why

The old saying that a picture is worth 1,000 words is true for logistic regression. It is beneficial to create graphs even if they are not included in your final paper. You can follow the `margins` command with the `marginsplot` command, which will automatically produce a graph of the results of `margins`.

Graphs help readers visualize data relationships. Admittedly, they get harder to interpret when they have three or more predictor variables. The graphs in this chapter do not account for interactions. Chapter 13 introduces interactions using logistic regression and shows how to generate graphs. In this chapter, we will illustrate graphs of

1. categorical predictors that include three or more categories,
2. one quantitative predictor,
3. one categorical predictor and one quantitative predictor,
4. a pair of categorical predictors, and
5. a pair of quantitative predictors.

11.2 Graphs of categorical predictors that include three or more categories

If the predictor is dichotomous, such as sex, a graph does not add much value after running the `margins` command. Graphs of categorical predictors make more sense when you have a predictor with more than two categories. The ordinal variable, `hlthstat`, has five categories, ranging from 1 for `Excellent` to 5 for `Poor`. You might treat this as a quantitative predictor variable, but we will treat it as a polytomous categorical predictor.

Let us open the working dataset we saved in chapter 10. We then use `recode` to reverse the coding of `hlthstat` so that our new variable, `hlthnew`, is coded from

1 for Poor to 5 for Excellent. This way, a higher score reflects the variable name. This clarifies whether it indicates better or worse health. This will minimize confusing explanations of the results.

```
. use "nhanes2l_working"
(Second National Health and Nutrition Examination Survey)
. recode hlthstat (5=1 "Poor") (4=2 "Fair") (3=3 "Good") (2=4 "Very good") ///
> (1=5 "Excellent"), generate(hlthnew) label(cat5)
(7,397 differences between hlthstat and hlthnew)
. label variable hlthnew "Self-reported health"
```

Note that we also labeled the hlthnew variable as "Self-reported health". Once we are satisfied with the variables and coding, we should save the dataset to include hlthnew:

```
. save "nhanes2l_working", replace
file nhanes2l_working.dta saved
```

Now we will run the logistic regression:

```
. logistic highbp age bmi i.female i.hlthnew, baselevels vsquish
Logistic regression                                     Number of obs =  10,335
                                                        LR chi2(7)    = 2424.86
                                                        Prob > chi2   =  0.0000
Log likelihood = -5828.298                              Pseudo R2     =  0.1722

------------------------------------------------------------------------------
      highbp | Odds ratio   Std. err.      z    P>|z|     [95% conf. interval]
-------------+----------------------------------------------------------------
         age |     1.0456   .0015472    30.13   0.000     1.042572    1.048637
         bmi |   1.145344   .0058389    26.62   0.000     1.133957    1.156846
      female |
        Male |          1  (base)
      Female |   .6119732   .0277564   -10.83   0.000     .5599196    .6688661
     hlthnew |
        Poor |          1  (base)
        Fair |   1.025771   .1004389     0.26   0.795     .8466509    1.242785
        Good |   1.070934   .0988874     0.74   0.458     .8936442    1.283395
   Very good |   .8591177    .081991    -1.59   0.112      .712553    1.035829
   Excellent |   .8691691   .0851751    -1.43   0.152      .717282    1.053219
       _cons |   .0033952   .0006169   -31.29   0.000      .002378    .0048475
------------------------------------------------------------------------------
Note: _cons estimates baseline odds.
```

The logistic regression reveals that no coefficient for hlthnew has a small p-value when the base level is Poor. These odds ratios (ORs) compare each of the Fair through Excellent groups with the Poor group. Based on this, we should not assume that hlthnew has no effect on the risk of high blood pressure. Because Poor was chosen as the base level, the output reports only tests for difference in odds between Poor and each of the other categories. We cannot tell from this output whether there may be differences among the other categories, as we might see if another base level were selected (see section 6.4). We get an overall test of a variable by using the testparm command (see section 14.2). It gives us a p-value for a joint test of all hlthnew coefficients.

```
. testparm i.hlthnew
 ( 1)  [highbp]2.hlthnew = 0
 ( 2)  [highbp]3.hlthnew = 0
 ( 3)  [highbp]4.hlthnew = 0
 ( 4)  [highbp]5.hlthnew = 0
           chi2(  4) =   17.75
         Prob > chi2 =    0.0014
```

This shows that the variable has an effect, $p = 0.001$.

Let us keep `Poor` as the base level and see how this works out. We will repeat the analysis using a different base level later.

We run the **margins** command to evaluate the average predicted probability of high blood pressure for each category of **hlthnew** based on the model we fit:

```
. margins i.hlthnew
Predictive margins                                    Number of obs = 10,335
Model VCE: OIM
Expression: Pr(highbp), predict()
```

	Margin	Delta-method std. err.	z	P>|z|	[95% conf.	interval]
hlthnew						
Poor	.4311919	.0160618	26.85	0.000	.3997115	.4626724
Fair	.4361318	.0107345	40.63	0.000	.4150925	.4571711
Good	.4445178	.0080548	55.19	0.000	.4287307	.460305
Very good	.4019494	.0088288	45.53	0.000	.3846453	.4192535
Excellent	.4041727	.0095473	42.33	0.000	.3854603	.4228852

Then, to plot the average predicted probabilities, we run

```
. marginsplot
Variables that uniquely identify margins: hlthnew
```

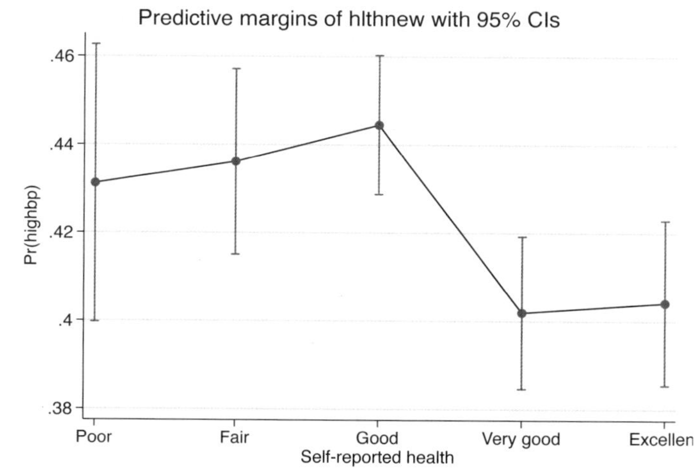

Figure 11.1. High blood pressure and self-reported health

Figure 11.1 shows that the relationship between the expected risk of high blood pressure and the level of self-reported health controlling for the other covariates is far from linear. There seems to be a big drop in the risk of high blood pressure for those who rate their health as very good or excellent compared with those who rate their health as good.

The 95% confidence bands around each point estimate in figure 11.1 show that there is little precision in our estimate of the average risk for the `Poor` category. A frequency distribution for `hlthnew` shows that there are 729 people out of 10,335 who said they had poor health—only 7% of the respondents, so estimates of statistics such as average risk for this category will not be estimated as precisely as they would if we had more data. The confidence band is much wider than the ones around the other categories that had far more people. Having few people in the `Poor` category will also make estimates of the odds imprecise. Therefore, when we use `Poor` as the base level in our logistic regression, we are unlikely to be able to detect differences in odds between `Poor` and the other categories. If we want to look for meaningful differences in odds, we might consider picking another category as the base level. If we want to draw conclusions directly from the logistic output, our selection of a base level should lead to comparisons that make sense. The `Good` category might be a good choice because it is at the center of the distribution of health and contains 2,938 people (28.4% of the total).

There are two ways to select `Good` as the base level and test for differences in odds of all other categories versus `Good`. We could use the `contrast` command:

```
. contrast rb3.hlthnew, effects or
Contrasts of marginal linear predictions
Margins: asbalanced

-------------------------------------------------------
                          |   df        chi2    P>chi2
--------------------------+----------------------------
                  hlthnew |
         (Poor vs Good)   |    1        0.55    0.4580
         (Fair vs Good)   |    1        0.39    0.5302
    (Very good vs Good)   |    1       12.64    0.0004
    (Excellent vs Good)   |    1       10.35    0.0013
                   Joint  |    4       17.75    0.0014
-------------------------------------------------------

------------------------------------------------------------------------------
              |  Odds ratio   Std. err.       z    P>|z|     [95% conf. interval]
--------------+---------------------------------------------------------------
      hlthnew |
        (Poor |
           vs |
        Good) |    .9337647   .0862216    -0.74   0.458     .7791832    1.119014
        (Fair |
           vs |
        Good) |    .9578284   .0657544    -0.63   0.530     .8372462    1.095777
   (Very good |
           vs |
        Good) |    .8022138   .0497338    -3.55   0.000     .7104267    .9058598
   (Excellent |
           vs |
        Good) |    .8115994   .0526731    -3.22   0.001     .7146584    .9216902
------------------------------------------------------------------------------
```

In this `contrast` command, `rb3.hlthnew` specifies that 3 (`Good`) should be used as the base level for `hlthnew`. The results show that the `Very good` and `Excellent` categories have lower odds of high blood pressure—OR $= 0.802$, $p < 0.001$ and OR $=$ 0.812, $p = 0.001$, respectively—when contrasted to the `Good` category.

An alternative is to refit the logistic regression model, changing the base level from category 1, `Poor`, to category 3, `Good`. We do this by inserting `ib3.hlthnew` into the command, signifying that `hlthnew` is a categorical variable and to use category 3 as the base level:

```
. logistic highbp age bmi i.female ib3.hlthnew, baselevels vsquish
Logistic regression                                    Number of obs =  10,335
                                                       LR chi2(7)    = 2424.86
                                                       Prob > chi2   =  0.0000
Log likelihood = -5828.298                             Pseudo R2     =  0.1722

------------------------------------------------------------------------------
      highbp | Odds ratio   Std. err.      z    P>|z|     [95% conf. interval]
-------------+----------------------------------------------------------------
         age |     1.0456   .0015472    30.13   0.000     1.042572    1.048637
         bmi |   1.145344   .0058389    26.62   0.000     1.133957    1.156846
      female |
       Male  |          1  (base)
     Female  |   .6119732   .0277564   -10.83   0.000     .5599196    .6688661
     hlthnew |
       Poor  |   .9337647   .0862216    -0.74   0.458     .7791832    1.119014
       Fair  |   .9578284   .0657544    -0.63   0.530     .8372462    1.095777
       Good  |          1  (base)
  Very good  |   .8022138   .0497338    -3.55   0.000     .7104267    .9058598
  Excellent  |   .8115994   .0526731    -3.22   0.001     .7146584    .9216902
       _cons |    .003636   .0005857   -34.87   0.000     .0026517    .0049858
------------------------------------------------------------------------------
Note: _cons estimates baseline odds.
```

Now we get more helpful information from the logistic regression. When we use `Good` as the base level for `hlthnew`, neither `Poor` nor `Fair` have a small p-value—0.458 and 0.530, respectively. However, those who report very good or excellent health have lower odds of high blood pressure, $p < 0.001$, than those with good health.

We saw that self-reported health had a significant effect when we used the `testparm` command, $p = 0.001$. Now we see that the significant effect becomes evident using `Good` as the base level. A reasonable conclusion is that self-reported health is associated with a lower risk of high blood pressure for those who self-report their health as very good or excellent. We did not find a reliable difference between self-reports of poor, fair, or good.

As you examine the graph in figure 11.1, notice that the range for the probability on the y axis is from 0.38 to 0.46. This narrow range could mislead anyone who should have paid more attention to it. Let us instead use a range from 0.20 to represent a low risk and 0.50 to represent a moderately high risk. The range in our graph should be consistent with what is known about the outcome based on existing literature. Otherwise, we will exaggerate or minimize the visualization of the effect. If we do not choose a reasonable range, we may fool some readers and irritate others by “misrepresenting” our results.

To make changes, we can use the Graph Editor, which we can open by clicking on the icon that looks like a bar graph and pencil at the top of the Graph window or by right-clicking anywhere in the graph and selecting **Start Graph Editor** from the drop-down menu.

1. Once the Graph Editor is open, double-click on the title, and a dialog box will appear. Delete the existing title text from the block labeled *Text:*. Click on **OK**.
2. Double-click on the *y*-axis title, and another dialog box will appear. Change the text in the *Text:* box to `Pr(High blood pressure)`. Click on **OK**.
3. Right-click on any number on the *y* axis, such as `0.42`. Click on **Axis properties**, and another dialog box will appear. Click on *Range/Delta*. Enter `0.20` for the *Minimum value*, `0.50` for the *Maximum value*, and `0.10` for the *Delta*. Click on **OK**.
4. Right-click on any value label on the *x* axis, such as `Good`. Click on **Axis properties**, and another dialog box will appear. Click on the **Label properties** button, change *Angle:* to `45°`, and ensure that the *Use value labels* box is checked. Click on **OK**.

To close the Graph Editor, right-click anywhere in the graph, select **Stop Graph Editor**, and then click on **Don't save**. Finally, right-click anywhere in the graph, click on **Copy**, and go to your document to paste it. Chuck Huber, Director of Statistical Outreach for StataCorp, has an excellent three-minute YouTube video (search for "Modifying graphs using the Graph Editor" on https://www.youtube.com). Here is the revised graph:

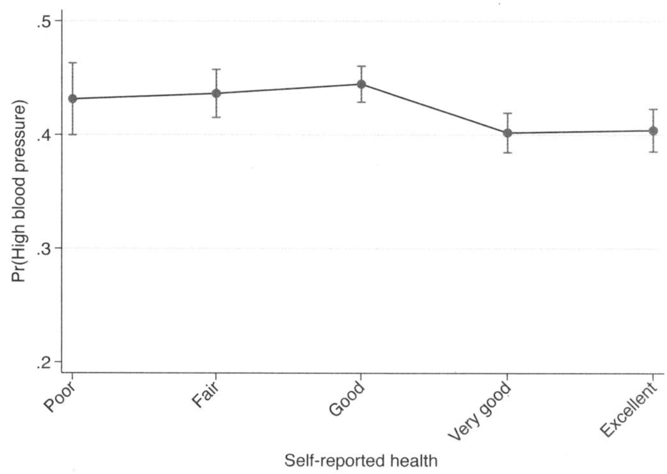

Figure 11.2. High blood pressure and self-reported health (edited)

11.3 Graphs with one quantitative predictor

The logistic regression showed an effect of body mass index (BMI) on the odds of high blood pressure (OR = 1.145, $p < 0.001$). The underlying research question likely is, "How does BMI affect the probability of high blood pressure?" To smooth the curve representing the effect of BMI, we can specify many values in the `margins` command. Let us use BMIs of 15, 20, 25, 30, 35, 40, 45, 50, 55, and 60. This smooths out the plot.[1]

1. If we were not making a graph, then we might prefer specifying fewer values.

```
. margins, at(bmi=(15(5)60))

Predictive margins                              Number of obs = 10,335
Model VCE: OIM

Expression: Pr(highbp), predict()
1._at:   bmi = 15
2._at:   bmi = 20
3._at:   bmi = 25
4._at:   bmi = 30
5._at:   bmi = 35
6._at:   bmi = 40
7._at:   bmi = 45
8._at:   bmi = 50
9._at:   bmi = 55
10._at:  bmi = 60

------------------------------------------------------------------------------
             |            Delta-method
             |     Margin   std. err.      z    P>|z|     [95% conf. interval]
-------------+----------------------------------------------------------------
         _at |
          1  |   .1660258    .0076168    21.80   0.000     .1510972    .1809544
          2  |   .2690771    .0065143    41.31   0.000     .2563093     .281845
          3  |   .4000603     .004736    84.47   0.000     .3907779    .4093427
          4  |   .5441095    .0066718    81.55   0.000      .531033    .5571859
          5  |   .6816487    .0099719    68.36   0.000     .6621041    .7011933
          6  |   .7959953    .0112247    70.91   0.000     .7739953    .8179953
          7  |   .8790467    .0100598    87.38   0.000     .8593298    .8987636
          8  |   .9325096    .0076248   122.30   0.000     .9175652     .947454
          9  |   .9638557    .0051492   187.19   0.000     .9537634    .9739479
         10  |   .9811171    .0032266   304.07   0.000     .9747931    .9874411
------------------------------------------------------------------------------
```

These results show a sharp increase in average predicted risk of high blood pressure as BMI increases, with the expected risk ranging from just 16.6% to near certainty at 98.1%, controlling for the covariates.

The `marginsplot` command produces a graph of the relationship between BMI and the risk of high blood pressure, shown in figure 11.3.

```
. marginsplot, title("") ytitle("Pr(High blood pressure)")
Variables that uniquely identify margins: bmi
```

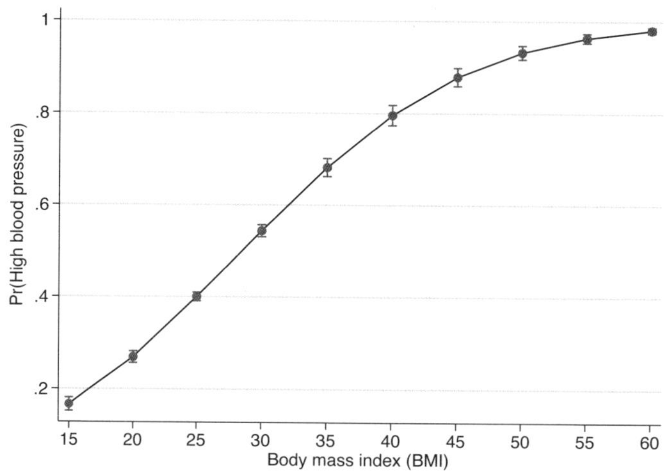

Figure 11.3. BMI and high blood pressure

The graph above is an excellent way to communicate the relationship between BMI and estimated risk of having high blood pressure. It is more explanatory and understandable than the raw logistic regression coefficients and OR, especially for a nontechnical audience. The curve for BMI does not have the dramatic zone of transition we saw in figure 5.1 when we used hypothetical data. Still, there is a steep increase in risk from a BMI of 20 to 40 and then a leveling off at very high BMIs. Contrast expected risk for those who have a low BMI of 20 to those who have a BMI of 40. The difference between these two risks is dramatic: 26.9% versus 79.6%! This graph clarifies the average risk of obesity. It also shows that a BMI even a few points lower results in a substantially lower risk of high blood pressure. Patients who are marginally obese may see the dramatic benefit of lowering their weight, even by just a few pounds. This graph provides a strong motivation to achieve a healthy weight.

11.4 Graphs with one quantitative and one categorical predictor

We have seen that there are gender differences in the risk and that the risk increases dramatically for people who have a high BMI. We can examine their combined effect on the average risk of high blood pressure. We use the `margins` command, placing the categorical variable, `female`, before the comma and the quantitative variable, `bmi`, after the comma in the `at()` option. This produces 30 separate estimates of the probability, one for each combination of gender and BMI:

```
. logistic highbp age bmi i.female i.hlthnew
  (output omitted)
. margins i.female, at(bmi=(15(2.5)50))
  (output omitted)
```

We then run the `marginsplot` command to produce a graph of these estimates:

```
. marginsplot, title("") ytitle("Pr(High blood pressure)")
Variables that uniquely identify margins: bmi female
```

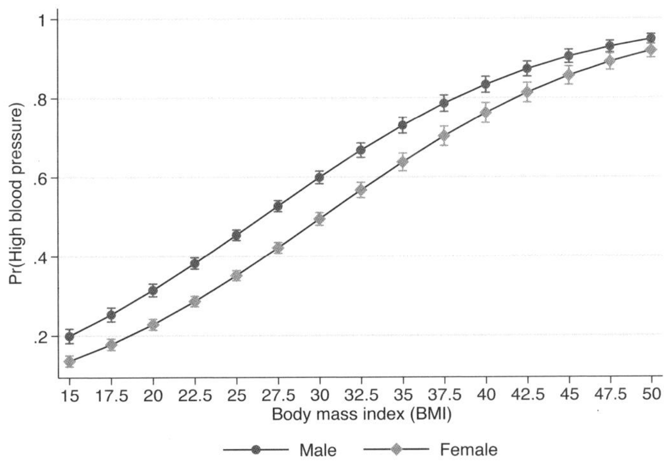

Figure 11.4. Effect of gender and BMI on high blood pressure

This graph shows the dramatic risk differences based on a person's BMI. The gender advantage of women gradually diminishes as both women and men approach Pr = 1.0 of high blood pressure for very high BMIs. Because logistic regression is linear when estimating the logits, the two lines would be equally distant from one another across the range if we plotted the estimated logits. However, when transformed into probabilities, the resulting lines converge at high BMIs. Note that we have treated the effects of sex and BMI as additive and have not allowed the lines to cross. We will compare this with what happens when we allow sex and BMI to interact in chapter 13.

11.5 Graphs of a pair of categorical predictors

Let us examine the combination of gender and self-reported health in predicting the risk of high blood pressure. Because both `hlthnew` and `female` are categorical variables, we specify `i.hlthnew#i.female` after the `margins` command. Here are the results for using both `female` and `hlthnew` as predictors, controlling for the covariates:

```
. logistic highbp age bmi i.female i.hlthnew
  (output omitted)
. margins i.hlthnew#i.female
  (output omitted)
```

We run `marginsplot` to produce a graph of these estimates:

```
. marginsplot, title("") ytitle("Pr(High blood pressure)") xlabel(, angle(45))
Variables that uniquely identify margins: hlthnew female
```

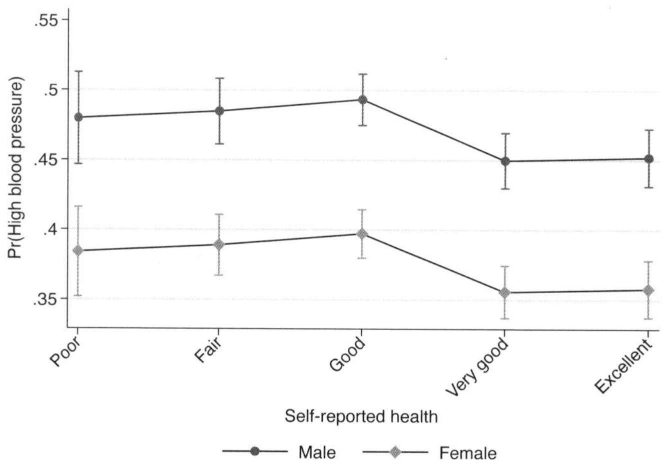

Figure 11.5. Effects of gender and self-reported health on high blood pressure

In chapter 13, we will consider incorporating an interaction effect.

11.6 Graphs with a pair of quantitative predictors

We can graph the additive effects of age and BMI by treating both as quantitative variables controlling for the covariates. We need to decide the number of values to specify for each predictor. For bmi, we will pick a lot of values by specifying at(bmi=(15(5)50) to get a smooth plot. We enter the bmi specification as our first quantitative variable. For age, we will pick just three values (20, 40, and 70) so that we have three lines—more lines would get confusing. Note that we place the variable with the fewest values (age) last in the margins command:

```
. logistic highbp age bmi i.female i.hlthnew
  (output omitted)
. margins, at(bmi=(15(5)50) age=(20 40 70))
  (output omitted)
```

We then run marginsplot to generate a graph of the results:

```
. marginsplot, title("") ytitle("Pr(High blood pressure)")
> plot1opts(msymbol(Oh) msize(large)) plot2opts(msymbol(Sh) msize(large))
> plot3opts(msymbol(dh) msize(large))
Variables that uniquely identify margins: bmi age
```

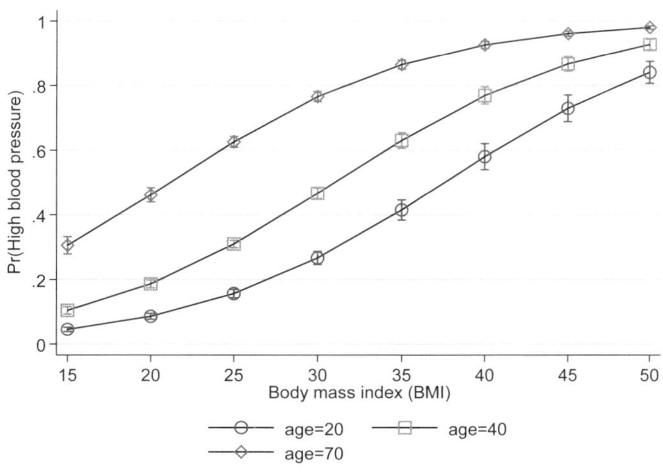

Figure 11.6. Effects of age with BMI on high blood pressure

This graph clearly shows how the average probability increases for people with higher BMIs and that this increase occurs whether they are young, middle-aged, or old. Incorporating interaction effects (chapter 13) would allow for a crossover of the curves between age and BMI. A young person who is in their 20s and has a low-to-normal BMI is unlikely to have high blood pressure. By contrast, a person who is morbidly obese is likely to have high blood pressure regardless of their age.

12 Curve fitting with quadratic models

Interpreting logistic regression results for quadratic models is more complicated than interpreting ordinary least-squares (OLS) linear regression results for quadratic models. We will review using a quadratic model for conventional OLS regression before applying a quadratic term with logistic regression.

In some cases, a strong argument can be made for fitting a curve rather than a straight line when using OLS regression to predict a quantitative outcome. We might predict that the effects of age on systolic blood pressure are modest for adults in their 20s. We might predict that age effects increase quickly from age 30 up to age 60 and that the age effects level off after age 60. To test this argument, a straight-line linear regression is inappropriate. You need to allow for a curve whenever you think the strength of a predictor's effect is contingent on the level of the predictor.

12.1 A hypothetical example of a quadratic model using OLS regression

Here is a seriously unrealistic but straightforward example. You have taught an Introduction to Statistics course 11 times. Your goal was to find the best session length. Each time you taught the course, the total time (number of meetings $\times$ length of each meeting) was the same. One time, you used many short meetings of 10 minutes. You even taught the course once using just a few 200-minute meetings. A very tough comprehensive test was given at the end of each course. It had a maximum possible score of 100.

We input and label the data below:

```
. input length score
          length       score
  1. 10 50
  2. 30 60
  3. 50 70
  4. 70 80
  5. 90 85
  6. 110 86
  7. 120 80
  8. 140 60
  9. 160 30
 10. 180 20
 11. 200 15
 12. end
. label variable length "Individual session length (minutes)"
. label variable score "Average score on final"
```

And then we list them below:

```
. list length score

     +----------------+
     | length   score |
     |----------------|
  1. |     10      50 |
  2. |     30      60 |
  3. |     50      70 |
  4. |     70      80 |
  5. |     90      85 |
     |----------------|
  6. |    110      86 |
  7. |    120      80 |
  8. |    140      60 |
  9. |    160      30 |
 10. |    180      20 |
     |----------------|
 11. |    200      15 |
     +----------------+
```

Let us visualize the shape of the relationship. As the length of the individual meetings increases from 10 minutes to 70 minutes, the test scores consistently increase. But for 70- to 110-minute sessions, the test scores level off. After 110 minutes, the test scores decrease quickly. If you have ever taken a class in statistics with extremely long sessions, you can appreciate the level of learning going down as the students doze off.

One way to visualize the relationship is to create a scatterplot. We use the `twoway` command and specify the `scatter` subcommand:

```
. twoway (scatter score length)
```

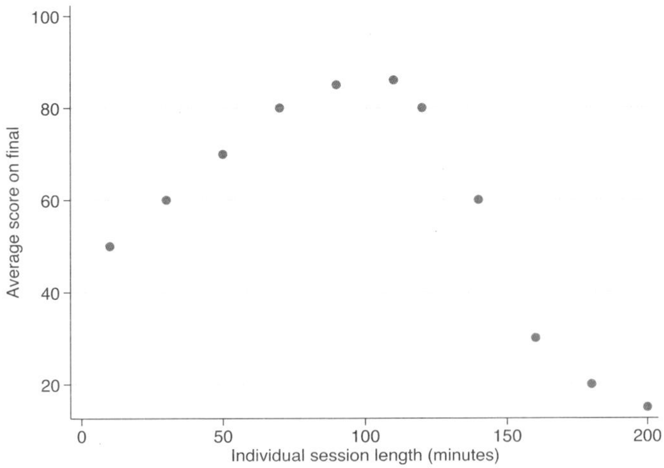

Figure 12.1. Length of sessions and test scores

When you have a large dataset, there will be hundreds or thousands of dots on the graph, which may disguise the relation's shape. In that case, a scatterplot is not applicable. One solution is to plot a lowess curve, which uses a nonparametric method that provides a locally weighted moving average. We run the `lowess` command:

```
. twoway (lowess score length)
```

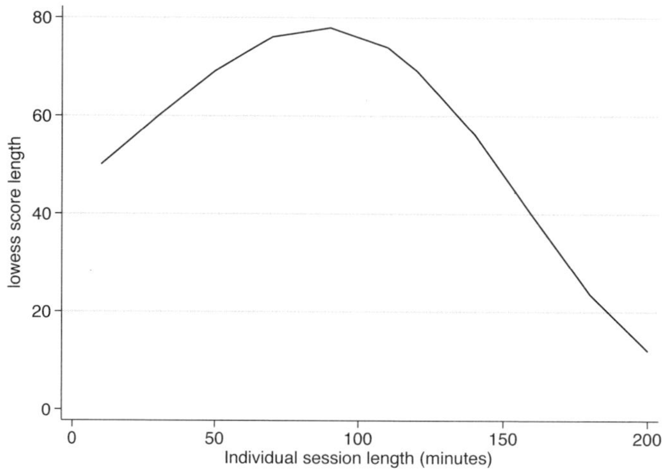

Figure 12.2. Length of sessions and test scores using a lowess curve

The lowess curve clarifies that OLS regression using a straight line will be a poor choice. How well will a linear model fit our hypothetical data?

```
. regress score length, beta
      Source |       SS           df       MS      Number of obs   =        11
-------------+----------------------------------   F(1, 9)         =      4.31
       Model |  2191.87271         1  2191.87271   Prob > F        =    0.0678
    Residual |  4581.76366         9  509.084851   R-squared       =    0.3236
-------------+----------------------------------   Adj R-squared   =    0.2484
       Total |  6773.63636        10  677.363636   Root MSE        =    22.563

------------------------------------------------------------------------------
       score | Coefficient  Std. err.      t    P>|t|                     Beta
-------------+----------------------------------------------------------------
      length |  -.2393112   .1153321    -2.07   0.068                -.5688486
       _cons |   83.05463   13.93564     5.96   0.000                        .
------------------------------------------------------------------------------
```

The results show $R^2 = 0.324$, $p = 0.068$; $B = -0.239$, $p = 0.068$; and $\beta = -0.57$. Without looking at the lowess curve, we could misinterpret the relationship. This OLS regression fails to capture what we saw in figures 12.1 and 12.2. The slope $B = -0.239$ shows that the estimated test score is lower by -0.239 points for each added minute of session time. That makes no sense for meeting lengths between 10 and 110 minutes. The $\beta = -0.569$ suggests a moderate-to-strong negative relationship. This also makes no sense given, the lowess curve. Before prematurely concluding that the courses with 10 minutes must have been great, we should put these graphs together. Figure 12.3 shows the plot of the actual data, the fit using a lowess curve, and the straight-line linear regression fit. We produced this two-way graph using the following command:

```
. twoway (lfit score length) (scatter score length) (lowess score length)
```

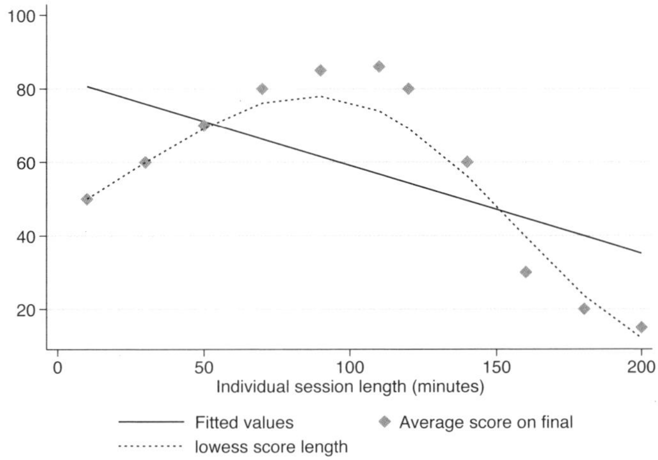

Figure 12.3. A linear regression provides a terrible and misleading fit to the data

Without looking at the data and adding a quadratic term, a researcher would jump to the erroneous conclusion that the shorter the individual sessions, the better. When we have large datasets, it is difficult to "look" at the data. This means that comparing a lowess curve with a linear fit is a good thing to do. The hypothetical data in this illustration are an extreme case where we need a curve to fit the relationship. Most real-world applications are less dramatic.

Far too many researchers fail to visualize the relationship. This can lead to badly misleading answers to research questions.

12.2 Estimating the curve (uncentered predictor)

There are two ways of adding a quadratic term to a model. First, I will show the uncentered approach, which includes the quadratic term directly:

$$y_i = a + B_1 x_i + B_2 x_i^2 + e_i$$

We could calculate the length squared variable by running the `generate lengthsq = length * length` command. Then we would enter both `length` and `lengthsq` in the model:

```
. regress score length lengthsq
```

But Stata has a quicker way. We can add a prefix of `c.` to the independent variable, acknowledging that it is a quantitative variable. When we use `c.length##c.length`, the two hash marks (#s) tell Stata to enter both **length** and the product, **length** squared, as predictors. If we included only one hash mark, only the product, **length** squared, would be included. Stata automatically generates the squared term for us. We run the following command:

```
. regress score c.length##c.length

      Source |       SS           df       MS      Number of obs   =        11
-------------+----------------------------------   F(2, 8)         =     35.25
       Model |  6083.39824         2  3041.69912   Prob > F        =    0.0001
    Residual |  690.238125         8  86.2797656   R-squared       =    0.8981
-------------+----------------------------------   Adj R-squared   =    0.8726
       Total |  6773.63636        10  677.363636   Root MSE        =    9.2887

------------------------------------------------------------------------------
       score | Coefficient  Std. err.      t    P>|t|     [95% conf. interval]
-------------+----------------------------------------------------------------
      length |   .9828624   .1880735     5.23   0.001     .5491642    1.416561
             |
   c.length#|
    c.length |  -.0058324   .0008684    -6.72   0.000     -.007835   -.0038298
             |
       _cons |   39.32404   8.678294     4.53   0.002     19.31186    59.33622
------------------------------------------------------------------------------
```

In contrast to the linear model of the same data, in which $R^2 = 0.382$, the quadratic model shows a much stronger effect of $R^2 = 0.898$, $p < 0.001$. Also, both **length** and **length** squared have small p-values. A small p-value for the quadratic term is strong evidence that we need to fit a curve. However, the quadratic term may still lack practical significance with a huge sample. This would be reflected in the R^2 for the model with the quadratic term being very close to the R^2 for the linear model.

Let us interpret the coefficients:

1. The intercept is 39.324. If **length** = 0, then **length** squared = 0, and all that is left in the model is the intercept. This is the estimated score for a nonexistent section that had zero-minute sessions, which are out of range of **length** (10–200 minutes). Therefore, any substantive interpretation would be questionable.

2. $B_1 = 0.983$ for **length** and $B_2 = -0.006$ for **length** squared. We should interpret these in combination rather than individually for the following reasons:

   a. At any point on the x axis, the estimated test score increases by 0.983 times **length** and simultaneously decreases by 0.006 times **length** squared.

   b. **length** and **length** squared are on different scales (10–200 compared with 100–40,000).

   c. We say that **length** and **length** squared are linked variables. Fortunately, Stata's **margins** command manages the linkage automatically (Long and Freese 2014) as long as we specify the model using **c.length##c.length**.

3. $B_1 = 0.983$ has an interpretation, but it is not very useful. It is the tangent of the curve at the intercept. It is not informative about any other point on the curve without simultaneously considering B_2.

Some people misinterpret B_1 and B_2. They assert that B_1 is the effect of `length` when `length` is small and that B_2 is the effect of `length` when `length` is large. Remember that both coefficients apply simultaneously, so it is problematic and misleading to interpret them as if they were independent variables. For small values of `length`, $B_1 = 0.983$ has a much bigger effect than the decrease because of the negative B_2 (-0.006) for `length` squared. For large `length` values, the B_2 for `length` squared becomes the dominant effect. Remember that the B_1 is multiplied by `length` (10, 30, 50, ..., 200). B_2 (-0.006) is multiplied by `length` squared (100, 900, 2,500, ..., 40,000). The dominance of B_2 as the squared value of `length` increases brings the curve back down. The regression results show that the plot goes up, levels off, and then drops as students and instructors get exhausted during extremely long sessions.

The problem of interpreting the relationship by looking at the Bs is complicated because `length` and `length` squared are measured on drastically different scales. We need a single scale. The most straightforward interpretation is the scale of the `length` variable itself, that is, 10 to 200 minutes. We do this with the `margins` command, specifying each of the possible lengths in the `at()` option to produce mean predicted scores. This estimated value combines the simultaneous linked effects. If we had a large dataset, we might run `margins, at(length=(10(10)200))`. With only 11 cases, we specify values to match our observed session lengths:

```
. margins, at(length=(10 30 50 70 90 110 120 140 160 180 200))
Adjusted predictions                                    Number of obs = 11
Model VCE: OLS

Expression: Linear prediction, predict()
1._at:  length =  10
2._at:  length =  30
3._at:  length =  50
4._at:  length =  70
5._at:  length =  90
6._at:  length = 110
7._at:  length = 120
8._at:  length = 140
9._at:  length = 160
10._at: length = 180
11._at: length = 200

-------------------------------------------------------------------------------
             |            Delta-method
             |     Margin   std. err.      t    P>|t|     [95% conf. interval]
-------------+-----------------------------------------------------------------
         _at |
          1  |   48.56942   7.156701     6.79   0.000     32.06604     65.0728
          2  |   63.56074   4.903129    12.96   0.000     52.25411    74.86738
          3  |   73.88614   3.866476    19.11   0.000     64.97003    82.80225
          4  |    79.5456   3.816484    20.84   0.000     70.74478    88.34643
          5  |   80.53914   4.050288    19.88   0.000     71.19916    89.87913
          6  |   76.86676   4.108529    18.71   0.000     67.39247    86.34104
          7  |   73.28084   4.034462    18.16   0.000     63.97736    82.58433
          8  |   62.60957    3.78347    16.55   0.000     53.88487    71.33427
          9  |   47.27237   3.832773    12.33   0.000     38.43398    56.11076
         10  |   27.26924   4.894111     5.57   0.001      15.9834    38.55508
         11  |   2.600181    7.17957     0.36   0.727    -13.95594     19.1563
-------------------------------------------------------------------------------
```

Because the outcome variable `score` is quantitative, the values in the `Margin` column are the mean predicted scores for each session length. The estimated average score for courses that include many 10-minute sessions is 48.569. The average score for 30-minute sessions, 63.57, is better. Notice how the average score increases rapidly as the session lengths get longer. This upward trend quits abruptly with session lengths of 90 minutes. After that, additional minutes of length result in lower scores and then dramatically lower scores.

The R^2 for the regression model, 0.898, shows that the quadratic model fits the data well. Compare the estimated means with the original data. For example, the course that used 10-minute sessions had an actual mean of 50; and the model predicts 48.569, showing that it provides a reasonably close fit to the original data. If we had other covariates in the model, the results would automatically adjust for those covariates.

We use `marginsplot` to help visualize the relationship between session length and predicted average test score:

```
. marginsplot, title("")
Variables that uniquely identify margins: length
```

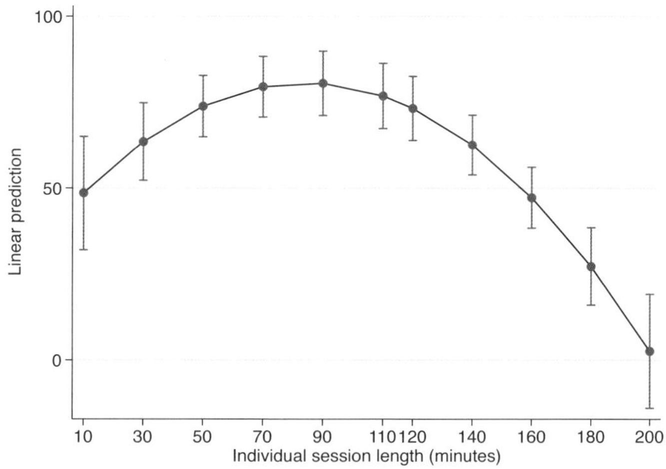

Figure 12.4. A curve showing the effect of a session length (uncentered)

The curve shows the relationship, allowing one to visualize precisely what happens to student performance in courses of varying length.

What is the ideal length of sessions? The `marginsplot` command indicates that it (peak of the curve) is between 70 and 90 minutes. We have only 11 different cases. With a strong R^2, we are confident in using the model to find the best length without being limited to the best length for which we have data. Can we narrow this down to an exact number of minutes in a session that maximizes learning? The value of `length` for which the `score` is maximized is

$$x = \frac{-B_1}{2\,(B_2)} = \frac{-0.98286}{2\,(-0.00583)} = 84.29331$$

We conclude that the optimal session length is 84.29331 minutes. The estimated learning increases with session length up to 84.29331 minutes and then drops back down. The 84.29331-minute session length is based on the quadratic solution.[1]

Now that we have decided on the best length of sessions to maximize the test score, we have one more question. At the hypothetical session length of 84.29331 minutes,

1. If the curve were ∪-shaped instead of ∩-shaped, this formula would let you find the value of the independent variable that results in the minimum value of the outcome variable.

what is the estimated average test score on the final? We insert 84.29331 as the value of `length` in the equation. The asymptotic value of the curve is

$$\widehat{y} = 39.32404 + 0.98286\,(84.29331) - 0.00583\,(84.29331^2) = 80.74830$$

The interpretation for the uncentered model is below:

> The longer individual sessions are, up to about 80 minutes, the more the students learn. However, as individual sessions get longer than 80 minutes, there is a gradual dropoff in performance followed by a steep dropoff in performance for very long sessions. This quadratic model explains 89.8% of the variances in how much students learn.

12.3 Centering, collinearity, and nonessential collinearity

Another approach involves centering the predictor by subtracting $\texttt{length}_i - M_{\texttt{length}}$, where $\texttt{length}_i$ is the length for the ith observation and $M_{\texttt{length}}$ is the mean length. The quadratic term is calculated by squaring the centered score $(\texttt{length}_i - M_{\texttt{length}})^2$. More generally, the centered quadratic model is

$$y_i = a + B_1(x_i - M_{x_i}) + B_2(x_i - M_{x_i})^2 + e_i$$

When we fit the uncentered model, we included two highly correlated terms. In our uncentered example, the r is 0.968 between length and length squared. If we center the length before squaring it, the correlation between the centered length and the centered length squared is -0.025.

We sometimes hear that we must center independent variables before squaring to avoid collinearity. You may even hear this from experienced journal editors. However, you do not need to center a variable before generating the quadratic. Both centered and uncentered approaches produce different but equivalent results. Neither has an advantage for obtaining convergence when using maximum likelihood estimation, so we can choose whichever approach provides the most straightforward interpretation based on our specific goals.

How is it possible that the collinearity does not matter? The answer is the distinction between essential and nonessential collinearity. The high correlation for uncentered quadratics creates nonessential collinearity or microcollinearity but not essential collinearity or macrocollinearity (Iacobucci et al. 2016). Stata can solve for the determinant of the covariance matrix equally well whether or not you center the variable first. This results in equivalent solutions. Nonessential collinearity results in a higher variance inflation factor, but this is not a problem when collinearity is nonessential (see section 15.1). However, centering affects only the result of a shift in scale. Because of this, Allison (2012b) concluded that nonessential collinearity has "no adverse consequences" for using a quadratic term or interaction term. We will illustrate the equivalence with an example.

12.4 Estimating the curve (centered x)

What changes if we center x? The best way to do so is the community-contributed command `center` (Jann 2004), which subtracts the mean from each score and generates a new variable with the prefix `c_`. For example, `length`, once centered, becomes `c_length`. You can download and install `center` by running

```
. ssc install center
checking center consistency and verifying not already installed...
installing into c:\ado\plus\ ...
installation complete.
```

First, we center `length` to generate the new variable `c_length`. Then we run the `summarize` command to see the result:

```
. center length
(generated variables: c_length)
. summarize length c_length

    Variable |        Obs        Mean    Std. dev.       Min        Max
-------------+---------------------------------------------------------
      length |         11    105.4545    61.86496         10        200
    c_length |         11    1.39e-06    61.86496  -95.45454   94.54546
```

Our 11 courses of Introduction to Statistics had a mean session length of 105.455 minutes and ranged from 10 to 200 minutes. When we center, we shift the location, so the mean becomes 0 (because of a rounding error, it is $1.39e-06$, that is, 0.00000139). The range of centered `length` is from a low of -95.455 minutes to a high of 94.545 minutes. This is a less intuitive way to measure session length.

We are now ready to run the regression. We will use the `c.` notation, making the ugly variable name of `c.c_length` for centered `length`:

```
. regress score c.c_length##c.c_length, vsquish

      Source |       SS           df       MS      Number of obs   =        11
-------------+----------------------------------   F(2, 8)         =     35.25
       Model |  6083.39824         2  3041.69912   Prob > F        =    0.0001
    Residual |  690.238125         8  86.2797656   R-squared       =    0.8981
-------------+----------------------------------   Adj R-squared   =    0.8726
       Total |  6773.63636        10  677.363636   Root MSE        =    9.2887

------------------------------------------------------------------------------
       score | Coefficient  Std. err.      t    P>|t|     [95% conf. interval]
-------------+----------------------------------------------------------------
    c_length |  -.2472455   .0474946    -5.21   0.001    -.3567683   -.1377228
 c.c_length#
  c.c_length |  -.0058324   .0008684    -6.72   0.000     -.007835   -.0038298
       _cons |   78.11111   4.119924    18.96   0.000     68.61055    87.61167
------------------------------------------------------------------------------
```

The intercept has a potentially valuable interpretation. It is the estimated test score when the centered length is 0. The centered length will be 0 when the length is at its mean, that is, 105.455 minutes. The intercept is the estimated test score for a course with average-length meetings. The intercept, `_cons` = 78.11, is the estimated average score for a class with an average session length of 105.455 minutes. This might be helpful information if the session lengths had been randomly sampled from all possible session lengths.

Consider predicting income from years of education. The estimated income for a person who has an average length of education would be the intercept. This estimate is for that exact length of education. With a strong curve, the estimate might differ sharply as you move away from the precise average length.

For the `margins` command, we need to pick values on the scale of the centered length, −95 minutes to a high of 95, corresponding to the uncentered values. We round to the nearest whole number after centering:

```
. margins, at(c_length=(-95 -76 -56 -36 -16 5 15 35 55 75 95))
Adjusted predictions                                    Number of obs = 11
Model VCE: OLS

Expression: Linear prediction, predict()
1._at:  c_length = -95
2._at:  c_length = -76
3._at:  c_length = -56
4._at:  c_length = -36
5._at:  c_length = -16
6._at:  c_length =   5
7._at:  c_length =  15
8._at:  c_length =  35
9._at:  c_length =  55
10._at: c_length =  75
11._at: c_length =  95
```

_at	Margin	Delta-method std. err.	t	P>|t|	[95% conf.	interval]
1	48.96195	7.093336	6.90	0.000	32.60469	65.31921
2	63.21378	4.949011	12.77	0.000	51.80134	74.62622
3	73.66642	3.878913	18.99	0.000	64.72164	82.61121
4	79.45315	3.810981	20.85	0.000	70.66501	88.24128
5	80.57394	4.045115	19.92	0.000	71.24589	89.90199
6	76.72907	4.106579	18.68	0.000	67.25928	86.19886
7	73.09013	4.0297	18.14	0.000	63.79763	82.38264
8	62.31281	3.778604	16.49	0.000	53.59934	71.02629
9	46.86957	3.843387	12.19	0.000	38.0067	55.73243
10	26.76039	4.933008	5.42	0.001	15.38486	38.13593
11	1.985295	7.24414	0.27	0.791	-14.71972	18.69031

These results are interpretable but could be more apparent because the range is not in minutes but in centered minutes. The estimated means do not match the uncentered estimates because we rounded the session lengths. For example, the 10-minute session shows −95 rather than −94.4545.

Now we run `marginsplot` to visualize the results:

```
. marginsplot, title("")
Variables that uniquely identify margins: c_length
```

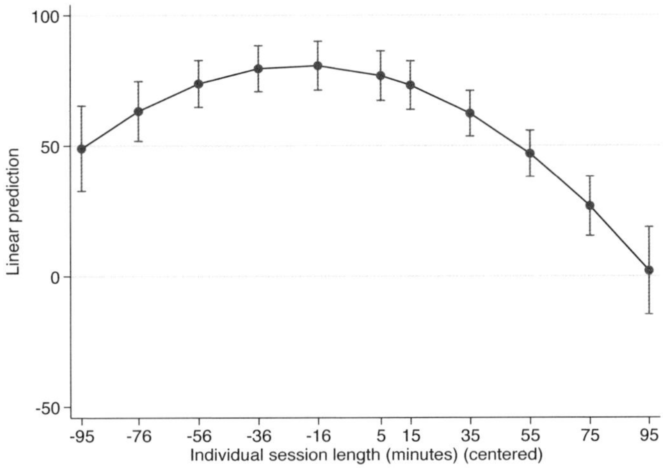

Figure 12.5. A curve showing the effect of centered session length on the score

The curve in figure 12.5 has the same shape as the uncentered curve in figure 12.4. It is harder for the reader to interpret because the centered `length` variable is no longer in minutes.

12.5 Compare centered and uncentered models

How are the centered and uncentered models alike?

1. The R^2 of 0.898, the $F(2,8)$ of 35.25, and the $p < 0.001$ are identical for both the centered and the uncentered models. The goodness of fit is unchanged.

2. Both `length` squared and centered `length` squared (`c_length*c_length`) have $B_2 = -0.0058$, $p < 0.001$. The effects of these product terms will always be identical whether or not you center.

3. The figures have identical shapes except for the shift in the `length` axis from minutes to centered minutes.

How are they different?

1. They use different scales on the x axis: the length of class meetings (10 to 200 minutes) versus the deviation from the average length (-95 to $+95$). The uncentered approach yields a more straightforward interpretation and visualization of the relationship.

2. The intercept for the uncentered model is the estimated score (39.324) at the out-of-range point of 0 on the length of the session scale. The intercept for the centered version (78.111) is for a test score for an average-length session (105.455 minutes).

3. The B_1 values for `length` are different. The B of 0.983 (uncentered version) is the tangent to the curve at `length` = 0.0. The B of -0.141 (centered version) is the curve's tangent at `c_length` = 0.0 when the length is at its mean. This is relevant only at 105.455 minutes and tells us that the test scores are going down at the exact point of 105.455 on the curve.

4. Although there are differences in the coefficients, interpreting them individually is not very useful because B_1 and B_2 should be interpreted simultaneously. The `margins` and `marginsplot` commands are the most helpful ways to interpret the model. Moreover, the interpretation is most straightforward for the uncentered solution.

Centering has no advantage if you are interested in the overall model and its ability to predict the outcome variable. If you are making a graphic presentation, centering makes the graph harder to interpret but does not change the shape of the relationship. B_1 and B_2 are linked variables, and neither of them tell you the rate of change along the plot. The best way to understand the nonlinear relationship is to use the `margins` command. If centering is more appropriate for your purposes, then you should also run the uncentered version and use that solution to create the graph.

12.6 Use of a quadratic with logistic regression

For logistic regression, we focus on the uncentered approach. If you prefer the centered approach, you can use the `center` command on your quantitative predictor (see section 12.4).

For illustrative purposes, we will predict whether a person has high blood pressure while controlling for the number of people living in their households. Logistic regression fits a linear model in terms of the natural log of the odds (the logit). Although having high blood pressure is a binary variable restricted to values of 0 and 1, the logit does not have this restriction. We will use a linear model to estimate the logit.

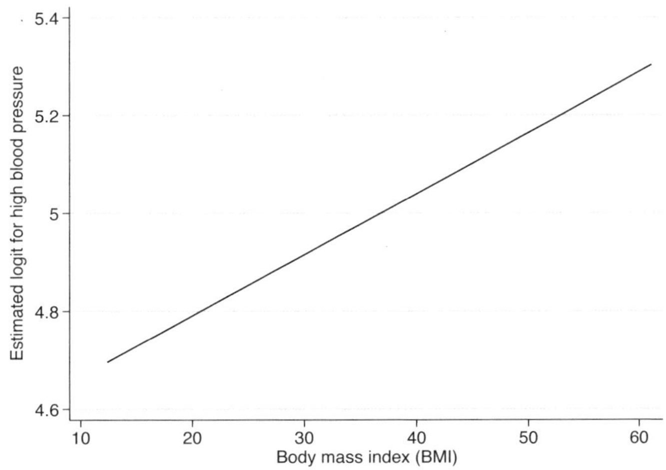

Figure 12.6. Estimated logit of high blood pressure predicted by BMI

Predicting the natural logarithm of the odds yields a straight-line prediction ranging from a logit around 4.7 to a logit around 5.3. Many people need help understanding logits. It helps to transform coefficients for predicting logits into odds ratios (see section 6.1). Better yet, we can transform predicted logits into predicted probabilities. At this point, we can estimate the probability of high blood pressure for specific levels of body mass index (BMI). We can also show the relationship between BMI and the probability of high blood pressure in a graph (figure 12.7).

Here is the series of commands:

```
. use "nhanes2l_working", clear
(Second National Health and Nutrition Examination Survey)
. logistic highbp c.bmi c.houssiz, vsquish
  (output omitted)
```

```
. margins, at(bmi=(15(5)60))

Predictive margins                                    Number of obs = 10,351
Model VCE: OIM

Expression: Pr(highbp), predict()
1._at:  bmi = 15
2._at:  bmi = 20
3._at:  bmi = 25
4._at:  bmi = 30
5._at:  bmi = 35
6._at:  bmi = 40
7._at:  bmi = 45
8._at:  bmi = 50
9._at:  bmi = 55
10._at: bmi = 60

------------------------------------------------------------------------------
             |            Delta-method
             |     Margin   std. err.      z    P>|z|     [95% conf. interval]
-------------+----------------------------------------------------------------
         _at |
          1  |   .1287218   .0063124    20.39   0.000     .1163497    .1410939
          2  |   .2393479   .0062798    38.11   0.000     .2270397    .2516561
          3  |   .4006633   .0050584    79.21   0.000     .3907489    .4105776
          4  |   .5863858   .0073042    80.28   0.000     .5720699    .6007017
          5  |   .7504368    .009512    78.89   0.000     .7317936    .7690801
          6  |   .8646908   .0086694    99.74   0.000     .8476992    .8816825
          7  |   .9315738   .0062648   148.70   0.000     .9192951    .9438525
          8  |   .9667322   .0039497   244.76   0.000     .9589909    .9744736
          9  |   .9841516   .0023003   427.83   0.000      .979643    .9886602
         10  |   .9925252   .0012777   776.81   0.000     .9900209    .9950294
------------------------------------------------------------------------------
```

We then run **marginsplot** to generate a graph of the results:

```
. marginsplot, title("") ytitle("Pr(High blood pressure)")
Variables that uniquely identify margins: bmi
```

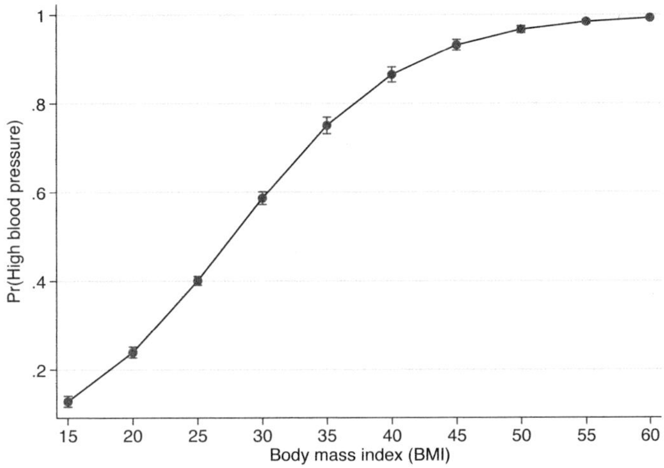

Figure 12.7. Estimated probability (additive model without quadratic term)

Figure 12.7 shows the expected risk of high blood pressure rapidly approaching certainty for higher BMI scores where it levels off. For the lowest BMI of 15, the average predicted probability of high blood pressure is 0.129 (based on the **margins** command). For the highest BMI of 60, the average predicted probability of high blood pressure is 0.993. Notice that the risk of high blood pressure is already over 90% for those with a BMI of 45 or higher. You may think the risk does not top out at a BMI of 45.

Let us examine the relationship using a quadratic model. You may think the risk of high blood pressure levels off before it reaches the near certainty shown in figure 12.7. Let us add a quadratic term for BMI. We illustrate only the uncentered approach. The centered approach produces the equivalent results except for a shift in the range of BMI, which in our uncentered data is 15 to 60. This range corresponds to being seriously underweight to morbidly obese.

```
. logistic highbp c.bmi##c.bmi c.houssiz, vsquish
Logistic regression                                     Number of obs =    10,351
                                                        LR chi2(3)    =   1230.29
                                                        Prob > chi2   =    0.0000
Log likelihood = -6435.6215                             Pseudo R2     =    0.0872

------------------------------------------------------------------------------
      highbp | Odds ratio   Std. err.      z    P>|z|     [95% conf. interval]
-------------+----------------------------------------------------------------
         bmi |   1.368041   .0453767     9.45   0.000     1.281933    1.459932
 c.bmi#c.bmi |   .9970826   .0005838    -4.99   0.000     .9959391    .9982275
     houssiz |   .8781973     .01139   -10.01   0.000     .8561546    .9008075
       _cons |   .0025078   .0011626   -12.92   0.000     .0010108    .0062218
------------------------------------------------------------------------------
Note: _cons estimates baseline odds.
```

These results show a negative quadratic effect because the odds ratio (OR) for $\text{BMI}^2 = 0.997$, $p < 0.001$ is less than 1.0. Remember not to dismiss the OR for bmi squared because it is so close to 1.0, and remember that this OR is multiplied by the bmi squared. For nhanes21.dta, the range of BMI is 15 to 60, but the range of bmi squared is 225 to 3,600.

It is best to interpret linked coefficients together rather than individually. For a given increase in a person's BMI, their OR is both increasing and decreasing. This is tricky to interpret, much less explain to a lay audience. We need to use the **margins** command to estimate the simultaneous effect of BMI and BMI^2:

```
. margins, at(bmi=(15(5)60))

Predictive margins                              Number of obs = 10,351
Model VCE: OIM

Expression: Pr(highbp), predict()
1._at:  bmi = 15
2._at:  bmi = 20
3._at:  bmi = 25
4._at:  bmi = 30
5._at:  bmi = 35
6._at:  bmi = 40
7._at:  bmi = 45
8._at:  bmi = 50
9._at:  bmi = 55
10._at: bmi = 60
```

	Margin	Delta-method std. err.	z	P>|z|	[95% conf.	interval]
_at						
1	.0904001	.0083144	10.87	0.000	.0741042	.1066959
2	.2212537	.0071327	31.02	0.000	.2072738	.2352336
3	.411685	.0055814	73.76	0.000	.4007456	.4226243
4	.5981258	.0075683	79.03	0.000	.5832921	.6129595
5	.7326382	.0099053	73.96	0.000	.7132242	.7520523
6	.8137836	.0149729	54.35	0.000	.7844374	.8431299
7	.857831	.0219026	39.17	0.000	.8149028	.9007592
8	.8781772	.0311475	28.19	0.000	.8171293	.9392251
9	.8816466	.0451248	19.54	0.000	.7932037	.9700896
10	.8694195	.0684474	12.70	0.000	.735265	1.003574

These results show a dramatic increase in the average risk of high blood pressure for each 5-point increase in BMI up to 40. With a BMI of 40, 81.4% of people are expected to have high blood pressure. The rate of increase in the risk slows after a BMI of 40. This is a sharp contrast to the results without the quadratic term, in which the estimated risk approaches certainty (greater than 0.900 for groups age 45 or older). With the quadratic term, the risk levels out at a lower probability.

Running **marginsplot** can help us visualize the relationship:

```
. marginsplot, noci title("") ytitle("Pr(High blood pressure)")
Variables that uniquely identify margins: bmi
```

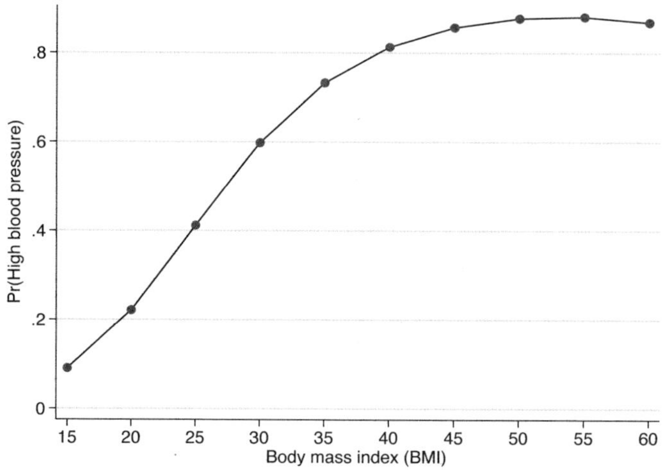

Figure 12.8. Estimated probability (quadratic model—uncentered)

If we center BMI, the **margins** and **marginsplot** commands switch the range to −13 to 32. The centered range makes interpreting the estimated probabilities and understanding the graph harder.

Here are the results for the centered version:

```
. center bmi
(generated variables: c_bmi)
. logistic highbp c.c_bmi##c.c_bmi c.houssiz, vsquish
  (output omitted)
. margins, at(c_bmi = (-13(5)35))
Predictive margins                                  Number of obs = 10,351
Model VCE: OIM

Expression: Pr(highbp), predict()
1._at:  c_bmi = -13
2._at:  c_bmi =  -8
3._at:  c_bmi =  -3
4._at:  c_bmi =   2
5._at:  c_bmi =   7
6._at:  c_bmi =  12
7._at:  c_bmi =  17
8._at:  c_bmi =  22
9._at:  c_bmi =  27
10._at: c_bmi =  32
```

	Margin	Delta-method std. err.	z	P>|z|	[95% conf.	interval]
_at						
1	.0531072	.0071531	7.42	0.000	.0390874	.067127
2	.1471673	.0083564	17.61	0.000	.1307891	.1635455
3	.3138048	.0056038	56.00	0.000	.3028216	.3247881
4	.5110357	.0066668	76.65	0.000	.497969	.5241024
5	.6737941	.0084627	79.62	0.000	.6572074	.6903807
6	.7795247	.0121812	63.99	0.000	.75565	.8033995
7	.8397766	.0182811	45.94	0.000	.8039464	.8756069
8	.8705451	.0261955	33.23	0.000	.8192029	.9218872
9	.8818517	.0374234	23.56	0.000	.8085032	.9552003
10	.8775316	.0553849	15.84	0.000	.7689792	.9860841

Let us run **marginsplot** to see the graph with the centered range:

```
. marginsplot
Variables that uniquely identify margins: c_bmi
```

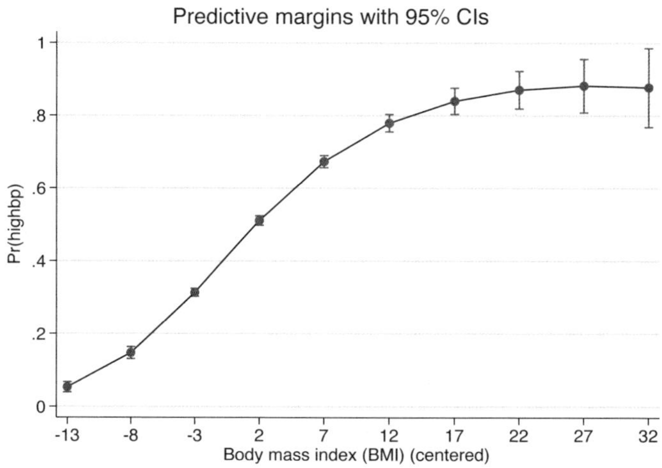

Figure 12.9. Estimated probability (quadratic model—centered)

The results for the centered solution are equivalent except for the shift in the scale of BMI. In this example, the uncentered version is preferred because it is easier to interpret the effect of BMI and BMI^2 on a familiar range of BMI scores than for the centered range. If you want to estimate the baseline odds for a person with an average score on the predictor, the value reported as the odds ratio for the intercept provides that for the centered version. Of course, you could also get this by using the **margins** command.

13 Interaction

13.1 Introduction

The effect of one variable can depend on the level of another variable. This is what statisticians mean by interaction. Using a quadratic term (see chapter 12) is a particular type of interaction. We found that the effect of body mass index (BMI) varied by the level of BMI. BMI had a strong effect up to about 40. For higher BMI values, we need to allow the consequence of BMI to dampen as the risk approaches its ceiling effect of 1.0. BMI interacts with itself. At low levels of BMI, there is a rapid increase in the risk of high blood pressure. By contrast, at high levels of BMI, the risk levels out.

We usually reserve the term *interaction* for when the effect of one variable is contingent on the level of a different variable. Consider the effects of age and gender on the risk of high blood pressure. With an additive model, we add the independent effects of age to the independent effects of gender to estimate the risk. What if age has more influence on high blood pressure for women? In that case, age and gender are linked variables; they are not genuinely independent. We need to allow for the contingent effect, so we add an interaction term.

It is helpful to think of predictors as a configuration. This configuration, not the variables acting independently, influences the outcome. The effect of one predictor is contingent on the level of another predictor, thus forming the configuration. This contingency effect is an old idea in statistical analysis; see, for example, Lazarsfeld (1958) and Acock and DeFleur (1972).

Qualitative researchers emphasize this approach, calling it *intersectionality*. By this, they mean that understanding the intersection of factors is critical, rather than the factors individually or adding up their independent effects. Examples of intersectionality include the effects of gender, education, and race as a configuration. Configurations of these factors are studied as sources of advantages and disadvantages. You must understand that the factors are linked. Quantitative researchers should also recognize the importance of configurations of variables and examine the effects using statistical interaction. The interacting variables are understood as linked variables rather than independent variables.

Here are three hypothetical examples of where both qualitative and quantitative researchers should consider interaction:

1. **Education achievement and gender to predict income.** Is the size of the payoff of additional education contingent on your gender? A three-way interaction might even be considered to examine the payoff of education by gender and race. Perhaps the increasing relative disadvantage women have from higher education is greater for Whites than it is for women who are not White.

2. **Religiosity and religious affiliation to predict political identification.** Greater religiosity may predict being conservative. This may vary widely across different religious affiliations; for some religious affiliations, greater religiosity may predict more liberal views.

3. **Participation in a Head Start program and the year in school to predict academic achievement.** Head Start participants might have a remarkable advantage during the earliest grades. Is the benefit of Head Start diminishing by the fifth grade?

In this chapter, we will fit models with possible interactions of

1. a categorical variable with a quantitative variable,
2. a pair of categorical variables, and
3. a pair of quantitative variables.

For interactions involving quantitative variables, we focus on uncentered quantitative variables. As explained in chapter 12, centering a quantitative variable reduces *nonessential collinearity* between the variable and its product (or between the variables that interact). Centering does not influence *essential collinearity*. Hence, centering merely shifts the location of the measurement scale of the independent variables. With interaction models, like quadratic models, the solution converges just as quickly whether or not you center variables. Furthermore, the overall fit and interaction are identical. The intercept and main effect have different interpretations because they apply to different points on the scale caused by the shift in the location. However, interpreting the size of the coefficients for the intercept applies only to one point on the distribution and is easily misinterpreted. If you find shifting the scale useful, you can center quantitative variables before generating the interaction term. This was demonstrated in chapter 12 using the community-contributed `center` command.

13.2 Interaction of a categorical and a quantitative variable using logistic regression

We will use `nhanes21_working.dta` with the modifications in section 11.2.

```
. use "nhanes21_working"
(Second National Health and Nutrition Examination Survey)
```

Our research question is as follows:

> Is the effect of age on the risk of high blood pressure different for women than men?

We predict the risk of high blood pressure (`highbp`) based on age and gender while controlling for household size. The `highbp` is coded as 1 if blood pressure is high and 0 otherwise. The `age` variable is the age measured in years. The `female` variable is coded as 1 if the person is female and 0 if male.

What is the result if we ignore the interaction between age and gender? Without an interaction term, we get

```
. logistic highbp i.female c.age c.houssiz
Logistic regression                                     Number of obs =  10,351
                                                        LR chi2(3)    = 1581.29
                                                        Prob > chi2   =  0.0000
Log likelihood = -6260.1218                             Pseudo R2     =  0.1121

------------------------------------------------------------------------------
      highbp | Odds ratio   Std. err.      z    P>|z|     [95% conf. interval]
-------------+----------------------------------------------------------------
      female |
      Female |    .653059   .0282323    -9.86   0.000      .6000041    .7108052
         age |   1.051251   .0015081    34.84   0.000      1.048299    1.054211
     houssiz |   1.059205   .0144625     4.21   0.000      1.031235    1.087934
       _cons |   .0673474   .0066237   -27.43   0.000      .0555398    .0816653
------------------------------------------------------------------------------
Note: _cons estimates baseline odds.
```

These results show that women have a lower risk of high blood pressure (OR $= 0.653$, $p < 0.001$). The risk of high blood pressure increases with age (OR $= 1.051$, $p < 0.001$) and household size (OR $= 1.059$, $p < 0.001$). However, we still need to answer our research question: does the effect of gender on the risk of high blood pressure vary by age? Quite the opposite; without an interaction term, this model assumes that there is no difference.

We can test for interaction by adding the product term of `age` $\times$ `female`. One way to estimate this effect is by generating a product term, `femaleXage`, and then including this interaction term in a logistic regression:

```
. generate femaleXage = female * age
. logistic highbp c.houssiz female c.age femaleXage
  (output omitted)
```

This will give us the correct parameter estimates. However, it will not allow us to estimate marginal predictions for combinations of gender and age. We need to use the `i.` for categorical variables and `c.` for quantitative variables. This also allows for just a single command:

```
. logistic highbp i.female##c.age c.houssiz
```

Notice the double hash marks (`##`), which mean that the categorical variable, `female`, and the quantitative variable, `age`, are included as main effects and that their product is also included.

```
. logistic highbp i.female##c.age c.houssiz, baselevels vsquish
Logistic regression                                 Number of obs =   10,351
                                                    LR chi2(4)    = 1702.81
                                                    Prob > chi2   =   0.0000
Log likelihood = -6199.3607                         Pseudo R2     =   0.1208

------------------------------------------------------------------------------
       highbp | Odds ratio   Std. err.      z    P>|z|     [95% conf. interval]
-------------+----------------------------------------------------------------
       female |
        Male |          1  (base)
      Female |   .1445957   .0211424   -13.23   0.000     .1085663    .1925819
         age |   1.037232   .0019023    19.93   0.000     1.033511    1.040967
female#c.age |
      Female |   1.030422    .002836    10.89   0.000     1.024878    1.035995
     houssiz |   1.075434   .0149026     5.25   0.000     1.046618    1.105043
       _cons |   .1233753   .0135807   -19.01   0.000     .0994331    .1530824
------------------------------------------------------------------------------
Note: _cons estimates baseline odds.
```

Trying to interpret the odds ratios (ORs) when you have an interaction is tricky and can lead to misunderstanding from ignoring the fact that the variables are linked. The main effect of `female` has OR $= 0.145$, $p < 0.001$. This OR is much less than 1.0, indicating that women have dramatically lower odds of high blood pressure. The main effect of `age` has OR $= 1.0372$, $p < 0.001$, indicating that the odds of high blood pressure increase with age. These interpretations ignore the linkage of age and gender because of their interaction.

The interaction `female#age` has OR $= 1.030$, $p < 0.001$. This effect indicates that the odds of high blood pressure increase more rapidly for women than men because the product term, `female` $\times$ `age`, drops out of the model for men; that is, `female#age` $=$ $0 \times$ `age` $= 0$ for men because men must have a score of 0 for `female`.

The effect of age for women includes the main effect of `age` times the interaction `female#age` effect: with ORs, we do not add the values; we multiply them ($1.037 \times 1.030 = 1.068$). We conclude that women's odds of high blood pressure increase with age faster than men's odds.

The results indicate that women have lower odds than men if we consider gender and age as independent variables. However, women's odds increase more with age than men's odds. It is not clear when or if women's odds catch up with men's odds across the range of age in our data.

The intercept `_cons` = 0.123, $p < 0.001$ is not useful for these data. It is the estimated baseline odds for an out-of-range man (`female` = 0) who is zero years old and is in a memberless household (`houssiz` = 0). The main advantage of centering is that the intercept estimates the baseline odds for a person who is precisely average on all variables, including the dubious meaning of having an average score on a dichotomous variable like `female`.

There is a vastly better and easier way to make sense of interaction! A less complicated and more understandable approach is to estimate and plot the average probabilities of high blood pressure by using the `margins` and `marginsplot` commands. It is much easier to interpret the effects by estimating them directly as probabilities of high blood pressure and plotting the result.

13.3 Estimating and interpreting probabilities (uncentered)

Because the uncentered version puts the results of the `margins` and `marginsplot` commands on the original scale of `age`, we will interpret only the uncentered version.

Because `female` is a categorical variable, we enter it before the comma in the `margins` command. After the comma, we enter the quantitative variable at specified ages. The effects of any additional covariates such as `houssiz` are controlled for because they are left at their observed values, and then predictions are averaged to obtain the reported margins.

```
. margins i.female, at(age=(20(10)70))

Predictive margins                                      Number of obs = 10,351
Model VCE: OIM

Expression: Pr(highbp), predict()
1._at: age = 20
2._at: age = 30
3._at: age = 40
4._at: age = 50
5._at: age = 60
6._at: age = 70

------------------------------------------------------------------------------
             |            Delta-method
             |     Margin   std. err.      z    P>|z|     [95% conf. interval]
-------------+----------------------------------------------------------------
  _at#female |
      1#Male |   .2416841    .010937    22.10   0.000     .2202481    .2631202
    1#Female |   .0776208   .0054728    14.18   0.000     .0668943    .0883472
      2#Male |   .3145153   .0096629    32.55   0.000     .2955764    .3334542
    2#Female |   .1405197   .0069217    20.30   0.000     .1269535     .154086
      3#Male |     .39775   .0080179    49.61   0.000     .3820353    .4134648
    3#Female |   .2409583   .0074856    32.19   0.000     .2262868    .2556297
      4#Male |   .4873371   .0074662    65.27   0.000     .4727036    .5019706
    4#Female |   .3812026    .007469    51.04   0.000     .3665636    .3958416
      5#Male |    .577752   .0088848    65.03   0.000     .5603381    .5951659
    5#Female |   .5444589   .0087955    61.90   0.000       .52722    .5616977
      6#Male |   .6632639   .0109923    60.34   0.000     .6417193    .6848085
    6#Female |   .6987415   .0104054    67.15   0.000     .6783474    .7191357
------------------------------------------------------------------------------
```

There is a huge disparity between women and men at age 20 (`1#Female` and `1#Male`) with the average probability of high blood pressure for women just 0.078 or a 7.8% risk compared with 0.242 or a 24.2% risk for men. The risk climbs steadily with age, regardless of gender. However, the risk for women starts to catch up with the risk for men. By the time people are 60, the average probability of high blood pressure for women is 0.544 (54.4% risk) compared with 0.578 (57.8% risk) for men.

To visualize the uncentered results, we run the `marginsplot` command:

```
. marginsplot, title("") ytitle("Pr(High blood pressure)")
Variables that uniquely identify margins: age female
```

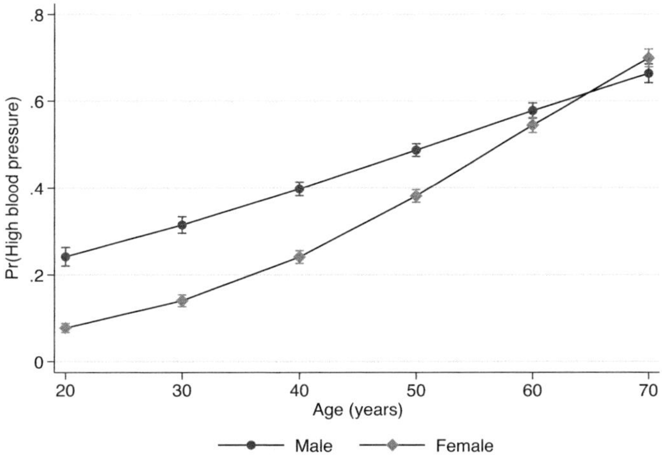

Figure 13.1. Interaction of gender and age predicting high blood pressure (uncentered)

If we did this for the centered version, the estimated probabilities and figure would be identical except for the shift in the scale for age. Instead of running from 20 to 70, the centered age would run from −27.580 to 26.420. Using the actual age range makes it easier to interpret the estimated risk and understand the graph. For many independent variables, such as attitudes or beliefs, the original scale is arbitrary, and this advantage of the uncentered approach is not important.

Plotting the diminishing gap (uncentered). The plot includes confidence intervals for each specific age we used: 20, 30, 40, 50, 60, and 70. We can calculate women's diminishing advantage by calculating the differences in the probabilities at each age point. Williams (2012) suggested plotting the difference as a single line. This line is based on the differences between Pr(high blood pressure women) and Pr(high blood pressure men) by age.

We use the `margins` command to compute the p-value for the gap at each age point. We add the `r.` operator, which requests reference category contrasts, to the binary `female` variable to obtain the differences in probabilities for men and women.

```
. margins r.female, at(age=(20(10)70))
Contrasts of predictive margins                    Number of obs = 10,351
Model VCE: OIM

Expression: Pr(highbp), predict()
1._at: age = 20
2._at: age = 30
3._at: age = 40
4._at: age = 50
5._at: age = 60
6._at: age = 70

------------------------------------------------------------
                    |         df        chi2     P>chi2
--------------------+---------------------------------------
          female@_at |
(Female vs Male) 1  |          1      186.71     0.0000
(Female vs Male) 2  |          1      221.62     0.0000
(Female vs Male) 3  |          1      207.69     0.0000
(Female vs Male) 4  |          1      100.97     0.0000
(Female vs Male) 5  |          1        7.21     0.0073
(Female vs Male) 6  |          1        5.69     0.0170
              Joint |          5    38060.61     0.0000
------------------------------------------------------------

---------------------------------------------------------------------------------
                    |             Delta-method
                    |   Contrast   std. err.     [95% conf. interval]
--------------------+------------------------------------------------------------
          female@_at |
(Female vs Male) 1  |  -.1640634   .0120069     -.1875965    -.1405302
(Female vs Male) 2  |  -.1739956   .0116877      -.196903    -.1510881
(Female vs Male) 3  |  -.1567917   .0108798     -.1781157    -.1354678
(Female vs Male) 4  |  -.1061345   .0105624     -.1268363    -.0854326
(Female vs Male) 5  |  -.0332931   .0124031     -.0576026    -.0089835
(Female vs Male) 6  |   .0354777   .0148683      .0063364      .064619
---------------------------------------------------------------------------------
```

The expected risk of high blood pressure is lower (Diff $= -0.164$, $p < 0.001$) for women than for men at age 20. Women's risk is even lower (Diff $= -0.174$, $p < 0.001$) at age 30. From there on, women's advantage diminishes until, by age 70, women have a slightly greater risk than men (Diff $= 0.035$ $p = 0.017$). A summary you could write to describe these points is as follows:

> Women's expected risk is substantially lower than men's expected risk when they are young, and the difference remains substantial until age 50. By age 60, women have just slightly lower risk. By age 70, women have a slightly greater risk of high blood pressure.

Finally, to see the same results graphically, we run **marginsplot** on the gender differences over age. Here we add a horizontal line at zero using the **yline(0)** option. A difference of zero means that there is no gender difference at that age. Women are advantaged by having a lower risk below this line; men are advantaged above this line.

```
. marginsplot, yline(0) title("") ///
> ytitle("Difference in risk of high blood pressure")
Variables that uniquely identify margins: age
```

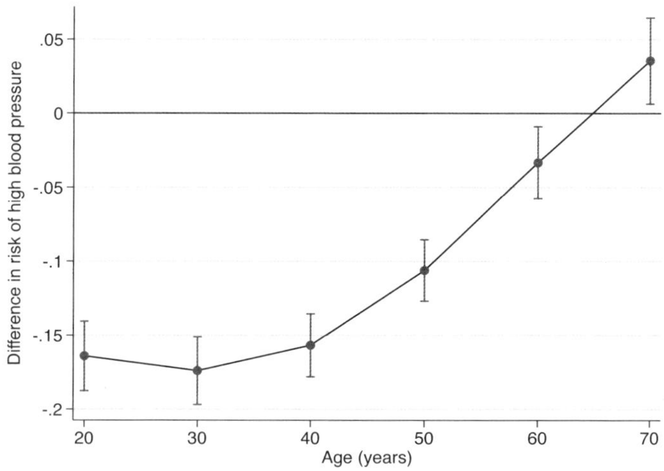

Figure 13.2. The large advantage of women decreases with age (uncentered)

Because **female** is binary, the **dydx()** option for the **margins** command, which we saw in section 10.4.1, produces the same results as using the **r.** operator. Thus, an alternative way to estimate the difference in the expected risk of high blood pressure for males and females for different ages, controlling for house size, is

```
. margins, dydx(female) at(age=(20(10)70))
  (output omitted)
```

How would we do this if we wanted to center **age**? Here is the set of commands we would use (results not shown):

```
. center age
. logistic highbp i.female##c.c_age c.houssiz, baselevel vsquish
. margins r.female, at(c_age=(-27.580(10)22.420))
. marginsplot
```

13.4 Interaction of categorical variables

What happens when we treat gender and self-reported health as linked variables? The `sex` variable (`female`) is coded as 0 for `Male` and 1 for `Female`. We will treat self-reported health as an ordinal categorical variable with five levels. In chapter 11, we recoded health status (`hlthstat`), creating the `hlthnew` variable coded so that a higher score signified better health: 1 for `Poor` to 5 for `Excellent`.

First, we run the logistic regression, including an interaction between `female` and `hlthnew`:

```
. logistic highbp i.female##i.hlthnew, baselevels vsquish
Logistic regression                                     Number of obs = 10,335
                                                        LR chi2(9)    = 498.37
                                                        Prob > chi2   = 0.0000
Log likelihood = -6791.5401                             Pseudo R2     = 0.0354

------------------------------------------------------------------------------
      highbp | Odds ratio   Std. err.      z    P>|z|     [95% conf. interval]
-------------+----------------------------------------------------------------
      female |
        Male |          1  (base)
      Female |   1.185647   .1781357     1.13   0.257     .8832179    1.591633
     hlthnew |
        Poor |          1  (base)
        Fair |   .9263588   .1177911    -0.60   0.547     .7220125     1.18854
        Good |   .8770637   .1022462    -1.13   0.260     .6979107    1.102205
   Very good |   .5856862   .0692473    -4.52   0.000     .4645421    .7384225
   Excellent |   .5173803    .061108    -5.58   0.000     .4104632    .6521472
     female#
     hlthnew |
 Female#Fair |   .8757734   .1576309    -0.74   0.461     .6154369    1.246235
 Female#Good |   .5510422    .092435    -3.55   0.000     .3966427    .7655443
    Female # |
   Very good |   .4942144    .084755    -4.11   0.000     .3531336    .6916586
    Female # |
   Excellent |   .3930485   .0689744    -5.32   0.000     .2786585    .5543958
       _cons |   1.247059   .1283885     2.14   0.032     1.019185    1.525881
------------------------------------------------------------------------------
Note: _cons estimates baseline odds.
```

This shows a consistent interaction between gender and each level of self-reported health compared with the base level of `Poor`. The only exception is for the `Fair` category. Interpreting the main effects of gender and health is misleading when there is an interaction. With interaction, you need to interpret the main and interaction effects simultaneously. For example, the main effect of `female` has OR $= 1.19$, $p = 0.257$. We should not misinterpret this as saying that women have 19% higher odds or that gender is unimportant because of the large p-value. To understand the risk for women, we need to combine the effects of gender and self-reported health. The effect of gender is contingent on self-reported health status. Rather than going through these calculations by hand, we run the `margins` command and consider the expected probabilities of high blood pressure:

```
. margins i.hlthnew#i.female
Adjusted predictions                              Number of obs = 10,335
Model VCE: OIM

Expression: Pr(highbp), predict()

------------------------------------------------------------------------------
             |            Delta-method
             |     Margin   std. err.      z    P>|z|     [95% conf. interval]
-------------+----------------------------------------------------------------
  hlthnew#   |
    female   |
  Poor#Male  |   .5549738   .0254271    21.83   0.000     .5051376    .6048101
Poor#Female  |   .5965418   .0263363    22.65   0.000     .5449236      .64816
  Fair#Male  |   .5360111   .0185597    28.88   0.000     .4996346    .5723875
Fair#Female  |   .5453586   .0161723    33.72   0.000     .5136616    .5770557
  Good#Male  |   .5223881   .0136453    38.28   0.000     .4956438    .5491323
Good#Female  |    .416771   .0123333    33.79   0.000     .3925981    .4409438
  Very good #|
       Male  |    .422094   .0141809    29.77   0.000        .3943     .449888
  Very good #|
     Female  |   .2997097   .0123414    24.28   0.000      .275521    .3238984
  Excellent #|
       Male  |   .3921725   .0137983    28.42   0.000     .3651283    .4192168
  Excellent #|
     Female  |   .2311688   .0124048    18.64   0.000     .2068559    .2554818
------------------------------------------------------------------------------
```

Then we run `marginsplot` for a visualization of the results:

```
. marginsplot, title("") ytitle("Pr(High blood pressure)") xlabel(, angle(45))
Variables that uniquely identify margins: female hlthnew
```

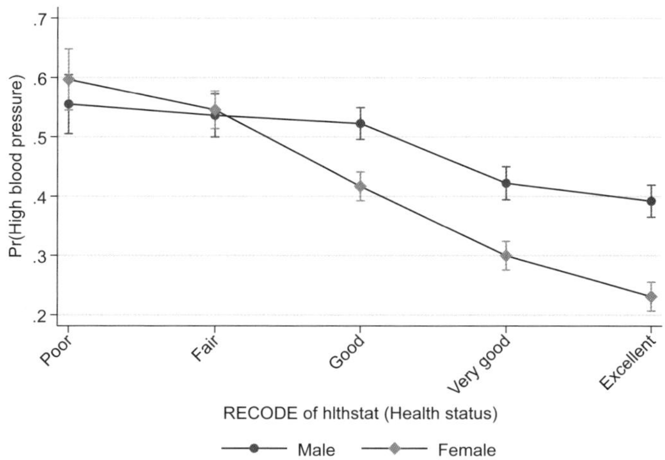

Figure 13.3. Interaction of gender and health predicting risk of high blood pressure

Figure 13.3 clarifies the interaction effect. The advantage women have is contingent on their self-reported health. Women have a substantially lower risk of high blood pressure than men if they both rate their health as good, very good, or excellent. Women are not advantaged over men when they report having poor or fair health.

Let us test the differences and obtain the *p*-values for the gender gaps. We will use the `r.` operator to do so. We will also use the `@` operator. Entering `r.female@hlthnew` tells Stata to report the tests for differences in expected probabilities across levels of female within (at) each level of `hlthnew`. Thus, we test for gender differences when `hlthnew` is `Poor`, `Fair`, `Good`, `Very good`, and `Excellent`. The `margins r.female@hlthnew` command is equivalent to running `margins r.female, at(hlthnew=(1(1)5))`.

```
. margins r.female@hlthnew

Contrasts of adjusted predictions                    Number of obs = 10,335
Model VCE: OIM

Expression: Pr(highbp), predict()

------------------------------------------------------------------
                               |         df        chi2     P>chi2
-------------------------------+----------------------------------
                female@hlthnew |
      (Female vs Male) Poor    |          1        1.29     0.2562
      (Female vs Male) Fair    |          1        0.14     0.7042
      (Female vs Male) Good    |          1       32.97     0.0000
 (Female vs Male) Very good    |          1       42.38     0.0000
 (Female vs Male) Excellent    |          1       75.30     0.0000
                         Joint |          5      152.08     0.0000
------------------------------------------------------------------

------------------------------------------------------------------------------------
                               |            Delta-method
                               |   Contrast   std. err.     [95% conf. interval]
-------------------------------+----------------------------------------------------
                female@hlthnew |
      (Female vs Male) Poor    |    .041568    .0366079     -.0301823     .1133182
      (Female vs Male) Fair    |   .0093476    .0246172     -.0389013     .0575964
      (Female vs Male) Good    |  -.1056171     .018393     -.1416668    -.0695674
 (Female vs Male) Very good    |  -.1223843    .0187991     -.1592299    -.0855386
 (Female vs Male) Excellent    |  -.1610037    .0185546       -.19737    -.1246374
------------------------------------------------------------------------------------
```

In the `Contrast` column, we see that the difference in risk of high blood pressure for women compared with men varies widely by the level of self-reported health. Women reporting poor or fair health have a similar risk to men. At the opposite extreme, women reporting excellent health have a substantially lower risk than men who report excellent health ($\text{Pr} = -0.161$, $p < 0.001$).

Finally, we run the **marginsplot** command, adding the optional horizontal line standing for no gender gap using **yline(0)**.

```
. marginsplot, yline(0) title("") ///
> ytitle("Difference in risk of high blood pressure") xlabel(, angle(45))
Variables that uniquely identify margins: hlthnew
```

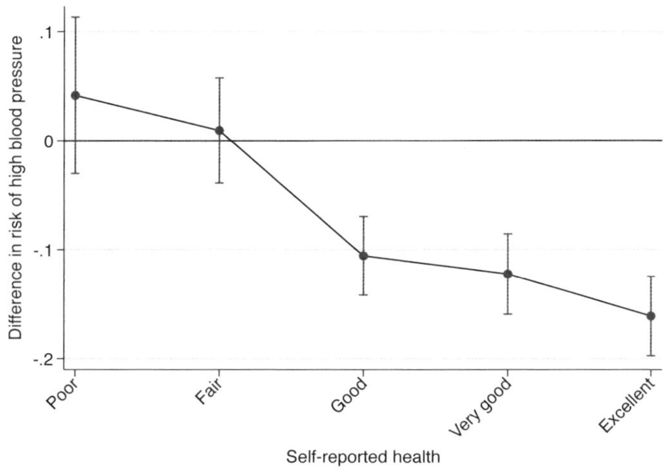

Figure 13.4. Women's advantage for those reporting good or better health

Again, we see that

1. Women have no advantage if their reported health is poor or fair.
2. Women have a substantial advantage if their reported health is good, very good, or excellent.

13.5 Interaction of quantitative variables

We will use three research questions to illustrate the interaction of a pair of quantitative variables:

1. What is the effect of age on the risk of high blood pressure?
2. What is the effect of BMI on the risk of high blood pressure?
3. Is there an interaction between age and BMI? Do different BMI risk groups have different trajectories of high blood pressure by age?

We can answer the first two questions assuming there is no interaction:

```
. logistic highbp c.age c.bmi

Logistic regression                                    Number of obs =  10,351
                                                       LR chi2(2)    = 2295.05
                                                       Prob > chi2   =  0.0000
Log likelihood = -5903.2393                            Pseudo R2     =  0.1628

------------------------------------------------------------------------------
      highbp | Odds ratio   Std. err.      z    P>|z|     [95% conf. interval]
-------------+----------------------------------------------------------------
         age |   1.046239   .0014489    32.64   0.000     1.043403    1.049083
         bmi |   1.145469   .0058173    26.74   0.000     1.134124    1.156928
       _cons |    .002455    .000372   -39.66   0.000     .0018242    .0033038
------------------------------------------------------------------------------
Note: _cons estimates baseline odds.
```

These results show that both age and BMI have a significant effect. For age, each additional year multiplies the estimated odds of high blood pressure by 1.046 (OR $=$ 1.046, $p < 0.001$). Each additional point on the BMI score multiplies the estimated odds of high blood pressure by 1.145 (OR $= 1.145$, $p < 0.001$).

When you have two quantitative predictors, specify just a few combinations. We will use ages 20, 35, 50, and 65 and BMIs of 20, 30, and 50. By entering the BMI levels last in the command, we will get a separate line for each BMI level when we produce the graph.

```
. margins, at(age=(20(15)65) bmi=(20 30 50))

Adjusted predictions                                    Number of obs = 10,351
Model VCE: OIM

Expression: Pr(highbp), predict()
1._at:  age = 20
        bmi = 20
2._at:  age = 20
        bmi = 30
3._at:  age = 20
        bmi = 50
4._at:  age = 35
        bmi = 20
5._at:  age = 35
        bmi = 30
6._at:  age = 35
        bmi = 50
7._at:  age = 50
        bmi = 20
8._at:  age = 50
        bmi = 30
9._at:  age = 50
        bmi = 50
10._at: age = 65
        bmi = 20
11._at: age = 65
        bmi = 30
12._at: age = 65
        bmi = 50
```

	Margin	Delta-method std. err.	z	P>|z|	[95% conf.	interval]
_at						
1	.0839923	.0043373	19.37	0.000	.0754914	.0924932
2	.2628596	.0100379	26.19	0.000	.2431858	.2825335
3	.8435821	.0172901	48.79	0.000	.8096942	.87747
4	.1529994	.0055392	27.62	0.000	.1421427	.1638561
5	.4126247	.0090582	45.55	0.000	.3948709	.4303786
6	.9139745	.0099488	91.87	0.000	.8944751	.9334739
7	.2624574	.0070836	37.05	0.000	.2485739	.276341
8	.5805197	.007596	76.42	0.000	.5656318	.5954076
9	.9544007	.0054557	174.94	0.000	.9437076	.9650938
10	.4121215	.0100309	41.09	0.000	.3924612	.4317817
11	.7316362	.0073785	99.16	0.000	.7171747	.7460977
12	.9763215	.0029499	330.96	0.000	.9705397	.9821033

We then run **marginsplot** to see the visualization:

```
. marginsplot, noci title("") ytitle("Pr(High blood pressure)")
Variables that uniquely identify margins: age bmi
```

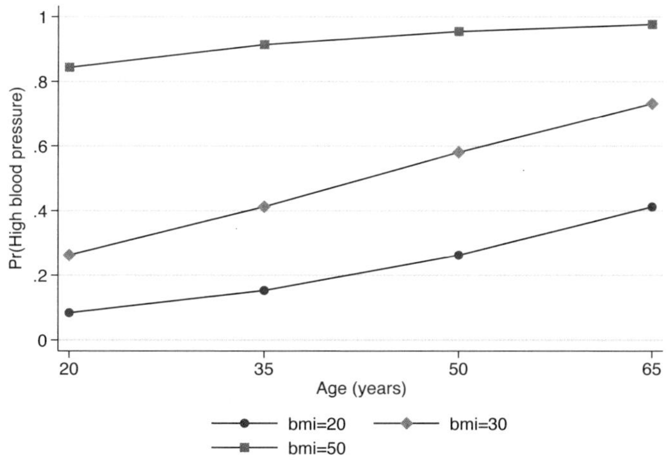

Figure 13.5. Age and BMI predicting risk without interaction

Without interaction, the three lines would be parallel when predicting logits. However, when predicting probabilities, the lines are no longer parallel. Thus, the effect of age on the probability of high blood pressure is contingent on BMI even without including an interaction term.

Our third question is whether there is an interaction between age and BMI. If the interaction term produces practically significant differences, then we need to interpret the results, including interaction.

```
. logistic highbp c.age##c.bmi
Logistic regression                                     Number of obs =  10,351
                                                        LR chi2(3)    = 2312.98
                                                        Prob > chi2   =  0.0000
Log likelihood = -5894.2736                             Pseudo R2     =  0.1640

------------------------------------------------------------------------------
      highbp | Odds ratio   Std. err.      z    P>|z|     [95% conf. interval]
-------------+----------------------------------------------------------------
         age |   1.081987   .0087559     9.74   0.000     1.064962    1.099285
         bmi |   1.221078   .0197094    12.37   0.000     1.183052    1.260325
             |
 c.age#c.bmi |   .9986809   .0003118    -4.23   0.000     .9980699    .9992922
             |
       _cons |   .0004815   .0002024   -18.17   0.000     .0002113    .0010973
------------------------------------------------------------------------------
Note: _cons estimates baseline odds.
```

Every coefficient has a p-value of less than 0.001. When there is an interaction, we need to assess the effects of age and BMI simultaneously because they are now linked rather than independent variables.

The interaction of age with BMI (OR $= 0.999$, $p < 0.001$) is close to 1.0. We might conclude that it has no practical significance. Before jumping to that conclusion, we need to remind ourselves of the distribution of the product term (`age` $\times$ `bmi`), which ranges from 240 to 4,514. This means that the interaction lowers the odds of high blood pressure by just a tiny amount per unit increase. But the product term has over 4,000 units with which to do this!

The intercept (`_cons`) of 0.0005 is not useful in this uncentered model, because it refers to the baseline odds for a nonexistent, out-of-range person who is 0 years old and has a BMI of 0. If we had centered age and BMI, the intercept would be the estimated baseline odds for a person of average age and BMI—a person who is precisely 47.580 years old and has a BMI of exactly 25.538. This may be valuable information in some applications, so we should first center on age and BMI. However, it is important to stress that the intercept is misleading if we try to apply it to anybody who is not very close to 47.580 years old with a BMI of close to 25.538. If the slopes are steep, there likely is a substantial difference, even with a slight divergence, from the exact means of the variables.

We will use the **margins** command to estimate the risk. We will use the same specific values for age and BMI that we used for the additive model.

```
. margins, at(age=(20(15)65) bmi=(20 30 50))

Adjusted predictions                              Number of obs = 10,351
Model VCE: OIM

Expression: Pr(highbp), predict()
1._at:  age = 20
        bmi = 20
2._at:  age = 20
        bmi = 30
3._at:  age = 20
        bmi = 50
4._at:  age = 35
        bmi = 20
5._at:  age = 35
        bmi = 30
6._at:  age = 35
        bmi = 50
7._at:  age = 50
        bmi = 20
8._at:  age = 50
        bmi = 30
9._at:  age = 50
        bmi = 50
10._at: age = 65
        bmi = 20
11._at: age = 65
        bmi = 30
12._at: age = 65
        bmi = 50
```

	Margin	Delta-method std. err.	z	P>|z|	[95% conf.	interval]
_at						
1	.0693991	.0049378	14.05	0.000	.0597213	.079077
2	.2967924	.0137337	21.61	0.000	.2698749	.3237099
3	.931122	.0165001	56.43	0.000	.8987825	.9634616
4	.1406426	.0060409	23.28	0.000	.1288027	.1524825
5	.4317716	.0103182	41.85	0.000	.4115483	.451995
6	.9424618	.0089667	105.11	0.000	.9248873	.9600363
7	.2642548	.007185	36.78	0.000	.2501725	.2783372
8	.5777067	.0075475	76.54	0.000	.5629139	.5924995
9	.9520308	.0057105	166.71	0.000	.9408384	.9632233
10	.440785	.0121966	36.14	0.000	.4168801	.4646899
11	.7112287	.0089415	79.54	0.000	.6937038	.7287536
12	.9600759	.0067567	142.09	0.000	.946833	.9733187

We will then run the marginsplot command to visualize the combination of effects.

```
. marginsplot, title("") ytitle("Pr(High blood pressure)")
> plot1opts(msymbol(Oh) msize(large)) plot2opts(msymbol(Sh) msize(large))
> plot3opts(msymbol(dh) msize(large))
Variables that uniquely identify margins: age bmi
```

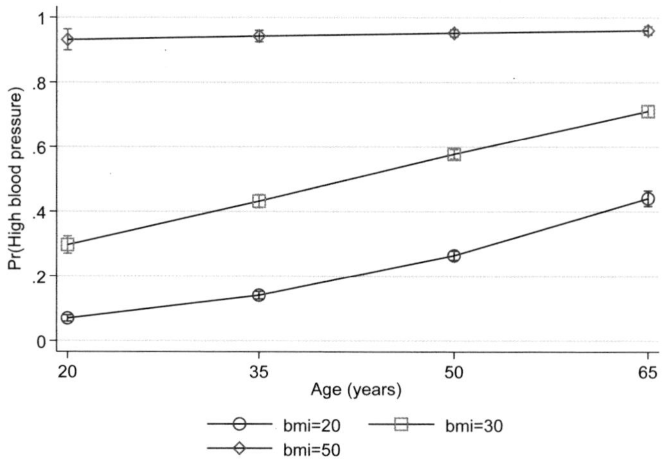

Figure 13.6. Age and BMI predicting with interaction

Figure 13.6 shows the following:

1. Morbidly obese people with a BMI $\geqslant$ 50 have an extremely high risk of high blood pressure across the age range (ceiling effect). Age has relatively little effect on this group. Compared with the additive model in figure 13.5, the interaction shows a high risk for those who are 20 years old.

2. For those who are marginally obese with a BMI of 30, the risk increases sharply with age.

3. For those with a low BMI of 20, their risk of high blood pressure increases slowly until they are approaching middle age and then increases at a rate like those who are marginally obese.

4. There is a substantial gap between BMI groups regardless of age.

14 Running nestreg and postestimation commands

Researchers often want to evaluate the need to add predictors to a model. Testing the addition of a single predictor is done by evaluating the p-value for the coefficient. If the single additional variable has a small p-value and is practically significant, you should add it. With ordinary least-squares (OLS) regression, the change in R^2 can identify practical significance. With logistic regression, the odds ratio (OR) can do so.

Instead of adding a single additional predictor, you may want to add a set of predictors simultaneously. Sociologists tend to start with predictors that are *ascribed* variables. For example, they might enter social class background, gender, and race as the first block of variables predicting which job candidates will be promoted. In a caste system, ascribed characteristics typically determine the outcome, and there is no need to add additional factors.

In countries that are liberal democracies, the sociologist would add achieved predictors as a second block. Examples of achieved characteristics include education, certifications, and marital status. Does the addition of this set of these achieved variables improve the model? To what extent do ascribed characteristics lose their importance when personal achievement variables are added? In a truly open society, the ascribed variables would drop out after adding the achieved variables.

After this, the sociologist might add a third group of variables, such as motivation and work-related attitudes. Does adding this third block improve prediction? Do the effects of ascribed and achieved variables become less vital after we add the third block? In a truly egalitarian society, the effects of ascribed characteristics would vanish after both the achieved characteristics and psychological values were added. You might have cross-cultural data. The relative importance of each block and each variable within each block will tell you a lot about each culture.

The way you group blocks of variables will depend on your field of study and training. A psychologist might start with a set of work attitudes, add a set of individual achievement variables such as education, and finally decide to add a set of control variables such as gender, race or ethnicity, and some geographic variables such as whether the person is in an urban or a rural area. The psychologist might want to show that the attitudes have an effect even after including the second and third blocks of variables.

Evaluating whether to add a set of variables involves a four-step process:

1. Fit the model with the original set of predictors.
2. Fit the model again, adding the second set of variables.
3. Evaluate the p-value of the additional set of variables to confirm that they make a unique contribution.
4. Interpret the ORs to see if adding the set of variables makes an important difference in the outcome.

Stata simplifies this process with the **nestreg** prefix command. The output is much more compact than the four-step approach. You will still want to take advantage of postestimation commands, such as **margins** and **marginsplot**, after running **nestreg**. I illustrate this process for logistic regression, but it can be used with various regression models.

14.1 Nested logistic regression

Nested modeling was originally called hierarchical modeling, and the name is still used in some research fields. However, calling it hierarchical modeling may be confusing because many people now use the term hierarchical modeling to refer to multilevel modeling, which involves using nested data. For example, student data are nested in classroom data, which are nested in school data. By contrast, in this section, we are using nested models to evaluate the addition of sets of variables to an existing model.

We will use `lbw_working.dta`, which we saved from chapter 1 to illustrate how to do nested regression. First, we will `clear` any open dataset and then run

```
. use "lbw_working"
(Hosmer & Lemeshow data)
```

Our outcome variable will be the newborn's low-birthweight status. Suppose that we have three prediction models from three hypothetical researchers: Dr. Rodriguez, Dr. Howahkan, and Dr. Smith. They have different ideas about what variables are needed to predict low birthweight. Dr. Rodriguez is passionately against smoking, especially for pregnant women. She runs a logistic regression by typing

```
. logistic low i.smoke
```

Dr. Rodriguez proudly publishes her results showing that a mother being a smoker dramatically doubles the risk of a low-birthweight newborn. In fact, she shows that the odds of a low-birthweight newborn about doubled if the mother smokes.

Dr. Howahkan says that smoking is an important predictor, but she is confident that it is not the only factor. She believes that adding a pair of risk factors, hypertension and race or ethnicity, will improve Dr. Rodriguez's model. She also believes that the addition of race and hypertension may dramatically weaken the adverse effect that Dr. Rodriguez reported for smoking. She fits her proposed model by typing

```
. logistic low i.smoke i.race i.ht
```

Dr. Smith says that all three variables (smoking, hypertension, and race) may be important predictors. However, we also must consider whether the mother frequently visited her doctor in the first trimester. He wants to add a single variable for this, `ftv`, that ranges from 0 to 6. The `fre` command shows that most of the new mothers did not have even a single visit with a doctor during their first three months of pregnancy. Running `summarize ftv` reports that the mean number of visits is only 0.794. He is worried that a variable with such little variance (standard deviation = 1.059) may not be as useful as he had hoped. Nonetheless, he decides to add `ftv` to the model and types

```
. logistic low i.smoke i.race i.ht c.ftv
```

When you learned OLS regression, you may have compared nested models by estimating the R^2 for each model. You may have then calculated an F test for the differences in R^2 and used the differences in the degrees of freedom to test each added set of variables. With logistic regression, we can test for a difference in nested models similarly. However, we use the difference in the likelihood-ratio χ^2 and difference in degrees of freedom with logistic regression.

Rather than running separate commands for each model, we use the `nestreg` prefix command. `nestreg` works whether you are doing OLS regression, logistic regression, or any of 18 other specialized types of regression. For each type of regression, it provides the appropriate tests. Using Stata's menu system, you can find `nestreg` buried under **Other** at the bottom of the **Statistics** menu. For logistic regression, we run

```
. nestreg, lrtable: logistic low (i.smoke) (i.ht i.race) (c.ftv), vsquish
```

The prefix command `nestreg` and its option `lrtable` (for likelihood ratio tests) are separated from the `logistic` command by a colon. Comparing the ideas of our three professors, we see that we have three levels. The first level includes smoking (Dr. Rodriguez). The second level adds both hypertension and race, while keeping the first level (Dr. Howahkan). The third level adds the frequency of medical visits during the first trimester (treated as a continuous variable) (Dr. Smith). Notice that each separate block is in parentheses and lists just the variables to be added to the model at that block.

Using `nestreg` gives us three solutions: one for just the first block, one for both the first and second blocks, and a final one including all three blocks. These individual results help us see what happens to variables in early blocks after adding the subsequent block or blocks. For example, does the effect of smoking increase or decrease when we add block two or three?

After reporting the three logistic models, a summary report shows the test statistic and *p*-value for a joint test of the predictors added in that block (comparing this model with the previous model):

```
. nestreg, lrtable: logistic low (i.smoke) (i.ht i.race) (c.ftv), vsquish
note: 0.smoke omitted because of estimability.
note: 0.ht omitted because of estimability.
note: 1.race omitted because of estimability.
Block 1: 1.smoke
Logistic regression                                     Number of obs =    189
                                                        LR chi2(1)    =   4.87
                                                        Prob > chi2   = 0.0274
Log likelihood = -114.9023                              Pseudo R2     = 0.0207

------------------------------------------------------------------------------
         low | Odds ratio   Std. err.      z    P>|z|     [95% conf. interval]
-------------+----------------------------------------------------------------
       smoke |
      Smoker |   2.021944   .6462989     2.20   0.028      1.08066    3.783112
       _cons |   .3372093   .0724103    -5.06   0.000     .2213694    .5136667
------------------------------------------------------------------------------
Note: _cons estimates baseline odds.
Block 2: 1.ht 2.race 3.race
Logistic regression                                     Number of obs =    189
                                                        LR chi2(4)    =  18.32
                                                        Prob > chi2   = 0.0011
Log likelihood = -108.17506                             Pseudo R2     = 0.0781

------------------------------------------------------------------------------
         low | Odds ratio   Std. err.      z    P>|z|     [95% conf. interval]
-------------+----------------------------------------------------------------
       smoke |
      Smoker |   3.094613   1.155269     3.03   0.002     1.488809    6.432408
          ht |
         Yes |   3.252896    2.02843     1.89   0.059     .9582541     11.0423
        race |
       Black |   2.803324   1.393428     2.07   0.038     1.058211    7.426326
       Other |    3.06541   1.240317     2.77   0.006     1.387004    6.774843
       _cons |   .1449379   .0525803    -5.32   0.000     .0711844    .2951068
------------------------------------------------------------------------------
Note: _cons estimates baseline odds.
```

```
Block 3: ftv
Logistic regression                                     Number of obs =    189
                                                        LR chi2(5)    =  18.49
                                                        Prob > chi2   = 0.0024
Log likelihood = -108.09321                             Pseudo R2     = 0.0788

------------------------------------------------------------------------------
         low | Odds ratio   Std. err.      z    P>|z|     [95% conf. interval]
-------------+----------------------------------------------------------------
       smoke |
     Smoker  |   3.075439   1.150067     3.00   0.003     1.477742    6.400527
          ht |
        Yes  |   3.197042   1.999656     1.86   0.063     .9383104    10.89306
        race |
      Black  |   2.793176   1.390427     2.06   0.039     1.052871    7.410058
      Other  |   3.020127    1.22772     2.72   0.007     1.361447    6.699611
         ftv |   .9391407   .1463022    -0.40   0.687     .6920347    1.274481
       _cons |   .1535948   .0598239    -4.81   0.000     .0715881    .3295432
------------------------------------------------------------------------------
Note: _cons estimates baseline odds.
```

Block	LL	LR	df	Pr > LR	AIC	BIC
1	-114.9023	4.87	1	0.0274	233.8046	240.2881
2	-108.1751	13.45	3	0.0038	226.3501	242.5588
3	-108.0932	0.16	1	0.6858	228.1864	247.6369

The `baselevels` option is unavailable when using `nestreg`. The base level for categorical variables is listed in the notes that appear immediately below the command. For example, the first note in the result is `0.smoke is omitted because of estimability`. This is an awkward way of saying that nonsmoker, coded as 0 for `smoke`, is the base level. The second note indicates that `No`, coded as 0 for `ht`, is the base level for hypertension. Finally, the third note indicates that `White`, coded as 1 for `race`, is the base level for that variable.

The first logistic regression model reports an overall model test with $\chi^2(1) = 4.87$, $p = 0.027$. The first block included `smoke`, which is practically significant with OR = 2.022, $p = 0.028$. Dr. Rodriguez is delighted!

The second block keeps `smoke` but adds both `ht` and `race`. Dr. Howahkan's model appears in block 2. This model, including blocks 1 and 2, reports an overall model test with $\chi^2(4) = 18.32$, $p = 0.001$. She is satisfied that race is practically significant, with both `Black` (OR $= 2.803$, $p = 0.038$) and `Other` (OR $= 3.065$, $p = 0.006$) having greater odds of high blood pressure than `White`. She is disappointed that hypertension does not have a lower p-value. Nonetheless, the hypertension variable, with OR $= 3.25$, $p = 0.059$, appears to have a strong effect. Dr. Howahkan recognizes that only 12 of 189 mothers report hypertension. Before concluding that hypertension is unimportant, Dr. Howahkan suspects that she needs a bigger sample size for adequate power. Her idea that smoking might be less predictive after race and hypertension were added to the model is unsupported. To her surprise, the OR for smoking is *increased* to OR $= 3.095$, $p = 0.002$ after race and hypertension are added to the model.

Dr. Smith thought he had a good idea and believed early prenatal care was critical. Block 3, which adds `ftv`, shows that `ftv` does not add to the model. The OR $= 0.939$, $p = 0.687$ for `ftv`. This p-value is very large. Dr. Smith, reluctant to give up, notes that the odds of a low-birthweight newborn drop by 6.1%$[(1 - 0.939) \times 100]$ for each added visit. The `ftv` variable is extremely skewed, with 93.7% of the cases scoring two or below. He speculates that he needs a much larger sample or a different way of coding the variable. He notes that just over half the mothers have no visit, so he might see about collapsing `ftv` into two or three categories.

At the bottom of the results is a summary table that shows the likelihood-ratio χ^2 testing of what each block adds. (Using `nestreg` with OLS regression, this table would also show each block's R^2 addition and F test.) For logistic regression, the table reports that for block 1, in which we just have `smoke` as our predictor, $\chi^2(1) = 4.87$, $p = 0.027$. This is the same as the χ^2 for the first model. The second block has $\chi^2(3) = 13.45$, $p = 0.004$. This test is for the *difference* between the first and the second model. (Do not confuse this with the χ^2 for the second model itself.) The third block has $\chi^2(1) = 0.16$, $p = 0.686$, for the difference between the second and third models.

Block	LL	LR	df	Pr > LR	AIC	BIC
1	-114.9023	4.87	1	0.0274	233.8046	240.2881
2	-108.1751	13.45	3	0.0038	226.3501	242.5588
3	-108.0932	0.16	1	0.6858	228.1864	247.6369

14.2 Selected postestimation commands

We often want to compare the effects of different variables or categories within a variable. A direct comparison makes sense only when the variables are measured on the same scale. It is not meaningful to directly test the difference between the effects of two variables if they are measured on different scales, such as gender versus income. Let us run a logistic regression predicting the probability of a low-birthweight newborn using whether the mother was a smoker, her race, and whether she was hypertensive.

```
. logistic low i.smoke i.race i.ht, baselevels vsquish
Logistic regression                                     Number of obs =    189
                                                        LR chi2(4)    =  18.32
                                                        Prob > chi2   = 0.0011
Log likelihood = -108.17506                             Pseudo R2     = 0.0781
```

low	Odds ratio	Std. err.	z	P>|z|	[95% conf.	interval]
smoke						
Nonsmoker	1	(base)				
Smoker	3.094613	1.155269	3.03	0.002	1.488809	6.432408
race						
White	1	(base)				
Black	2.803324	1.393428	2.07	0.038	1.058211	7.426326
Other	3.06541	1.240317	2.77	0.006	1.387004	6.774843
ht						
No	1	(base)				
Yes	3.252896	2.02843	1.89	0.059	.9582541	11.0423
_cons	.1449379	.0525803	-5.32	0.000	.0711844	.2951068

```
Note: _cons estimates baseline odds.
```

These results show that the odds of low birthweights for both the `Black` and the `Other` categories differ substantially from the odds for the base level of `White`. Compared with `White`, `Black` has OR = 2.803, $p = 0.038$; `Other` has OR = 3.065, $p = 0.006$. Is the effect of `Other` different from the effect of `Black`? Is an OR of 3.065 statistically different from an OR of 2.803? Both are different from the base level of `White`, but this does not answer the question of whether they are different from each other.

We use the `contrast` command, setting the base level of `race` to `Black` (`b2.race`) immediately after running the logistic regression. We want the effects using ORs, so we include the `effects` and `or` options:

```
. contrast b2.race, effects or
Contrasts of marginal linear predictions
Margins: asbalanced
```

	df	chi2	P>chi2
race	2	8.77	0.0125

	Odds ratio	Std. err.	z	P>|z|	[95% conf.	interval]
race						
(White vs base)	.3567194	.177312	-2.07	0.038	.1346561	.9449908
(Other vs base)	1.093491	.5460494	0.18	0.858	.4109192	2.909874

The (Other vs base) row has an OR = 1.093, $p = 0.858$. Because we have set the base level to Black, this OR reports Other having just slightly greater odds, but the very large p-value indicates that this is not a reliable difference. This lack of reliability is especially clear in the 95% confidence intervals, where the OR ranges from 0.411 to 2.910.

The (White vs base) row has an OR = 0.357, $p = 0.038$. This result reverses the order from the logistic regression. In the logistic regression, we found that Black has an OR = 2.803, $p = 0.038$, meaning much higher odds compared with White. When Black is the base level, in the contrast command, the OR = 0.357, $p = 0.038$, meaning that White has much lower odds compared with Black. Looking at the results in detail, notice that both ORs have the identical $|z| = 2.07$ and $p = 0.038$. Indeed, you might have noticed that the OR when Black is the base is the inverse of the OR when White is the base, that is, $1/2.803 = 0.357$.

Hypertension and smoking are binary variables measured with the same response categories: Yes or No. We can test whether their effects differ from each other. Rather than testing whether smoke and ht are different from having no effect (OR = 1.0), we want to compare the effect of smoking with the effect of hypertension. We can use the test command to test whether the coefficients on smoke and ht are equal.

```
. test 1.smoke = 1.ht
 ( 1)  [low]1.smoke - [low]1.ht = 0
           chi2(  1) =    0.00
         Prob > chi2 =    0.9444
```

Our null hypothesis is that there is no difference between the effect of smoking and the effect of hypertension. We can make this hypothesis because both smoking and hypertension are measured as binary variables. There is a large p-value, 0.944. We find no evidence that there is a difference in their effects. Remember, there were only 12 mothers who had hypertension. With few observations, it may be hard to detect an effect unless the effect is extremely strong.

Let us consider a different logistic regression model to test a set of categories. We will use a different dataset for this. We will type `clear` to discard the data we have open, and then we will open `nhanes2l_working.dta`. We are interested in regional differences in the risk of high blood pressure. We will include `region` as the primary interest but add `age` and `race` as covariates. The `region` variable represents the region of the US where a study participant lives. Here is a frequency distribution for `region`:

```
. use "nhanes2l_working", clear
(Second National Health and Nutrition Examination Survey)
. fre region
region — Region
```

		Freq.	Percent	Valid	Cum.
Valid	1 NE	2096	20.25	20.25	20.25
	2 MW	2774	26.80	26.80	47.05
	3 S	2853	27.56	27.56	74.61
	4 W	2628	25.39	25.39	100.00
	Total	10351	100.00	100.00	

The logistic regression results look very different depending on our chosen base level. If we use `i.region` in our model, the Northeast will be the base level. Alternatively, we might believe the Midwest is great because you believe that the Midwest is a low-key place to live, resulting in the lowest risk of high blood pressure. If you choose the Midwest, you would use `ib2.region` as the base level. Consider these two ways, `i.region` and `ib2.region`, of selecting the base level:

```
. logistic highbp i.region age race, baselevels vsquish
Logistic regression                                     Number of obs =  10,351
                                                        LR chi2(5)    = 1509.93
                                                        Prob > chi2   =  0.0000
Log likelihood = -6295.8028                             Pseudo R2     =  0.1071
```

highbp	Odds ratio	Std. err.	z	P>|z|	[95% conf.	interval]
region						
NE	1	(base)				
MW	.8607199	.0544316	-2.37	0.018	.7603826	.9742973
S	.8735282	.0549734	-2.15	0.032	.7721622	.9882009
W	.9041435	.057855	-1.57	0.115	.7975722	1.024955
age	1.04899	.001393	36.02	0.000	1.046263	1.051724
race	1.423986	.0765489	6.58	0.000	1.281587	1.582209
_cons	.0525855	.0054139	-28.61	0.000	.0429766	.0643429

```
Note: _cons estimates baseline odds.
```

```
. logistic highbp ib2.region age race, baselevels vsquish
Logistic regression                                    Number of obs =  10,351
                                                       LR chi2(5)    = 1509.93
                                                       Prob > chi2   =  0.0000
Log likelihood = -6295.8028                            Pseudo R2     =  0.1071

------------------------------------------------------------------------------
      highbp | Odds ratio   Std. err.      z    P>|z|     [95% conf. interval]
-------------+----------------------------------------------------------------
      region |
         NE  |   1.161818   .0734729     2.37   0.018     1.026381    1.315127
         MW  |          1  (base)
          S  |   1.014881   .0593876     0.25   0.801     .9049101    1.138216
          W  |    1.05045   .0627755     0.82   0.410      .934345    1.180983
         age |    1.04899    .001393    36.02   0.000     1.046263    1.051724
        race |   1.423986   .0765489     6.58   0.000     1.281587    1.582209
       _cons |   .0452614   .0046256   -30.29   0.000     .0370458    .0552991
------------------------------------------------------------------------------
Note: _cons estimates baseline odds.
```

Both models have the same overall model fit [$\chi^2(5) = 1509.93$, $p < 0.001$]. The ORs for age and race are identical in both solutions. By contrast, the ORs and p-values for regional differences reflect very different individual tests.

When we use the Midwest as the base level, only the odds for the Northeast differ from the odds for the Midwest. This illustrates the importance of the base-level choice.

What about the overall effect of the region? So far, we have been comparing individual regions with the base level. However, we have not tested the overall effect of region as a set of variables where each variable is a region.

To evaluate the overall importance of `region`, we could use the `nestreg` command, entering `i.region` as a block. Alternatively, we can use the `testparm` postestimation command, which tests if the three ORs for `region` (Midwest, South, and West) are all equal to 1.0 (when compared with the Northeast). Given that two of these three ORs have small p-values compared with the Northeast as the base level, you might assume that we could reject the null that all three ORs are jointly 1.0. However, the `testparm` results show that we do not have evidence to support this expectation, $p = 0.087$. Although we got very different OR results when we used the Midwest as the base, the `testparm` command produced the same result. We cannot justify that `region` has an effect overall. Here are both tests:

```
. quietly logistic highbp i.region age race, baselevels vsquish
. testparm i.region
 ( 1)  [highbp]2.region = 0
 ( 2)  [highbp]3.region = 0
 ( 3)  [highbp]4.region = 0
           chi2(  3) =    6.57
         Prob > chi2 =    0.0870
. quietly logistic highbp ib2.region age race, baselevels vsquish
. testparm ib2.region
 ( 1)  [highbp]1.region = 0
 ( 2)  [highbp]3.region = 0
 ( 3)  [highbp]4.region = 0
           chi2(  3) =    6.57
         Prob > chi2 =    0.0870
```

Regardless of how we select the base level, the test for the overall effect of `region` is the same.

15 Special topics

15.1 Collinearity and multicollinearity

Regression is sensitive to collinearity. If two variables are highly correlated, it is impossible to separate their independent effects because of two problems. First, with extreme collinearity, the maximum likelihood model may not be able to converge to a solution. Second, if there is a solution, the standard errors may be so large that a potentially important effect will be statistically significant only if you have an enormous sample N. In other words, you will need more power to show that even a substantial effect is statistically significant. If you have a sufficiently large N to obtain small standard errors and a satisfactory p-value, there remains a concern. The estimated coefficients and odds ratios you obtain can be either larger or smaller than they would have been without collinearity. In fact, they can even be in the opposite direction.

Multicollinearity means that a variable is so highly correlated with the set of covariates in the model that you have the same two problems. Extreme multicollinearity can happen even if none of the individual correlations between predictors is large, pair by pair.

Suppose that we generated a new variable measuring age in years and months, `agem = age * 12`. Because $r_{\texttt{age,agem}} = 1.0$, the logistic regression model (`logistic low age agem`) cannot converge to a solution with both age variables. Instead, with this extreme collinearity, Stata will try to find a solution by dropping a variable.

Let us load `lbw_working.dta` from chapter 1:

```
. use "lbw_working"
(Hosmer & Lemeshow data)
. generate agem = age*12
```

Here are the results:

```
. logistic low c.age c.agem, vsquish
note: agem omitted because of collinearity.
Logistic regression                                     Number of obs =    189
                                                        LR chi2(1)    =   2.76
                                                        Prob > chi2   = 0.0966
Log likelihood = -115.95598                             Pseudo R2     = 0.0118

         low   Odds ratio   Std. err.       z    P>|z|     [95% conf. interval]

         age     .9501333    .0299423    -1.62   0.105      .8932232    1.010669
        agem            1   (omitted)
       _cons        1.469    1.075492     0.53   0.599      .3498129    6.168901

Note: _cons estimates baseline odds.
```

If a pair of independent variables is highly but not perfectly correlated, the `logistic` command will not drop one of the variables, but it is still hard to separate their independent effects. One approach to check for this type of collinearity would be to examine all the pairwise correlations. For example, if a model includes `ht` and `lwt`, we could specify `correlate ht lwt` and find that $r = 0.236$.

15.1.1 Evaluating multicollinearity

A valuable way to check for multicollinearity is to calculate the variance inflation factor (VIF) for each predictor by using the `estat vif` command. This does not work directly after the `logistic` command. We can still get the results by first running an ordinary least-squares (OLS) regression. This may seem odd, but multicollinearity involves only the independent variables, so using the `estat vif` command after the OLS regression will report the level of multicollinearity for each predictor whether we are running OLS regression or logistic regression. See a discussion of this approach in the lecture notes of Richard Williams at https://www3.nd.edu/~rwilliam/stats2/l11.pdf.

First, run OLS regression including all the predictor variables we have in our logistic regression:

```
. quietly regress low i.smoke age c.lwt i.ht c.ftv i.race
```

Second, run the `estat vif` postestimation command:

```
. estat vif

    Variable |       VIF       1/VIF
-------------+----------------------
     1.smoke |      1.16    0.863333
         age |      1.13    0.883145
         lwt |      1.22    0.816601
        1.ht |      1.08    0.927069
         ftv |      1.07    0.930421
        race |
           2 |      1.19    0.839472
           3 |      1.34    0.747149
-------------+----------------------
    Mean VIF |      1.17
```

The `1/VIF` column reports how much variance in each variable is *unexplained* by the other predictors. Consider `age`. If we did a multiple regression of `age` on all the other independent variables (`regress age i.smoke lwt i.ht c.ftv i.race`), the R^2 would be 0.117. Hence, $1-0.117 = 0.883$[1] is the proportion of the variation in age that is unexplained by the other predictors. Age has a lot of independent variance when making an estimate. The `1/VIF` column shows that there is no problem with multicollinearity. If a predictor were completely independent of the other predictors, its VIF would be 1.00. A rule of thumb for potential multicollinearity is that it may be present any time the VIF is larger than 10.0, meaning less than 10% of the variance in the variable is independent of the other predictors.

A VIF of 10 should not be treated as an absolute, rigid cutoff (O'Brien 2007). Allison (2012a) points out that multicollinearity inflates the standard errors for the coefficients and can reverse the direction of the ORs. Suppose that you have a relatively small sample, $N = 100$, with a VIF of 15. Unless there is perfect multicollinearity, increasing the sample size to $N = 10000$ will reduce the standard errors dramatically, but your VIF will still be 15.

Depending on your application, you may focus on predicting the outcome without concern for the individual coefficients. Extreme collinearity makes interpreting the coefficients problematic. For example, two predictors correlated $r = 0.95$ have almost identical relations to the outcome when treated one at a time. If you enter both variables (`logistic y x1 x2, or`), you may get ORs in the reverse direction (one OR far below 1.0 and the other far above 1.0). However, if you are interested only in prediction, you may choose to ignore how much individual variables contribute.

1. The ratio 1/VIF for `age` is 0.885 rather than 0.883. Stata uses double precision in calculations, which explains the inconsistency.

Interaction products and squared variables result in high VIFs unless you center the variable or variables before computing the squared variable or interaction term. However, the squared variable or interaction product should still be included if they are theory driven and statistically significant. Section 12.3 discusses the difference between essential collinearity and nonessential collinearity. According to Allison (2012b), the nonessential collinearity for a quadratic or interaction term is manageable.

When there is a high level of multicollinearity, there are a few steps we can take. (Beginning researchers tend to include many predictors in highly complex models.) One solution is to drop variables with a high VIF, say, larger than 10. If several variables are highly correlated, we might do a principal component analysis and replace the variables with their scores on the principal component.

We might want to know whether mothers' or fathers' education better predicts their child's grade point average. Because of homogamy in mate selection, mothers and fathers have highly correlated education. We would need a large sample to get reliable estimates of their separate effects. Even with a large sample, the estimated coefficient may be misleading. They could be larger, smaller, or even in the opposite direction than they would be if there were no multicollinearity. It might be necessary to eliminate the mothers' or the fathers' education. Alternatively, we might use their sum or average as a single variable to represent parents' education, and then tell our readers that estimating reliable separate effects with a huge sample may be possible.

15.2 Sample size

In designing a research study, we need the power to identify effects that are true in the population and strong enough to have practical significance. If the sample is too small, we may find that a variable with a practically significant effect has a large p-value. With a very large sample, we would be wasting resources. There is no justification for the cost of a sample of 10,000 when a sample of 1,000 has adequate power. Also, many published studies have huge samples that report statistically significant results when the effects are too small to be considered practically significant. We should not ascribe importance to a result with a small p-value without evaluating the effect size. Unfortunately, this mistake is too common when working with very large samples.

Standards for how much power is adequate vary across fields of study. Some fields expect 90% power, but 80% power is more widely used as the standard. What does this mean? Suppose that we do a study of a new drug's effectiveness treating peripheral neuropathy. Let us say that we have 80% power. We find that the drug does not reduce the level of disease based on the p-value being greater than 0.05, so we decide to give up on it. With 80% power, there is a 20% risk that an effective drug is going to be deemed ineffective.

How many cases do you need to have 80% power? With OLS multiple regression with a quantitative outcome, there is a common rule of thumb in which you need at least 10 cases per predictor. This rule is highly debatable, but most importantly, it does not apply to logistic regression. You might see a rule of thumb for logistic regression that you need at least 300 cases to have adequate power. Long and Freese (2014) say that 300 cases may be large enough or that 500 cases are usually enough. Several factors are complicating estimating the N you need. Logistic regression uses maximum likelihood estimation. This is a large-sample procedure compared with OLS estimation. For maximum likelihood estimation, you need about 300 cases to test your overall model. If strong power is not critical, you might get by with 100 cases for a model with just a few predictors.

With OLS regression models, the power is not dependent on the mean of the dependent variable, because the variance of a normal distribution is independent of its mean. This is not the case for binary outcomes because the variance of a binary outcome is a function of the mean. With a rare event that happens only in 2% of the population, there may be too few cases of the event without a gigantic sample. Even with $N = 300$, your sample's expected number of events is only 6. The variance of a binary outcome is maximized when 50% of a population has the effect and 50% does not. Thus, it would be best to have more cases with rare events than the rules of thumb suggest. For rare events, even an N of 1,000 might have too little power.

One of our models (see section 14.1) included hypertension (`ht`) as an independent variable. Although $N = 189$, only 6.3% (12 cases) had hypertension. Thus, we do not have as much power for a test on the effect of this individual variable as we do for tests on others. By contrast, 39.2% (74 cases) smoked, and we had more power to test the effect of smoking. The key takeaway from this comparison is that when there are multiple predictors in a model, then those that are relatively rare, such as hypertension, will have a larger p-value for a given effect size.

We should also consider the distinction between the overall model's power and the individual predictors' power. The correlations among the predictors strongly influence your power. We have more power for a given sample size if the predictors are orthogonal. In section 15.1.1, we discussed a way to estimate the VIF. Unfortunately, most studies include several correlated predictors. This is critical if you need to calculate the power for a test of an odds ratio (OR) for an individual predictor.

Stata recently introduced a new command for performing a power analysis logistic regression. In the May 2025 StataNow update, the `power logistic` command can be used to estimate the needed sample size. It focuses on the key predictor, which is referred to as x. The command allows for covariates, referred to as z's. The outcome variable is referred to as y.

This command is explained in the Stata documentation. Particularly, the *Power and Sample-size Reference Manual* is over 850 pages, with over 70 pages specifically on the `power logistic` command and options. You are encouraged to explore the capabilities of `power logistic` for your research. Because the command is necessarily complex, it is good to consult a statistician with expertise in power analysis.

A detailed presentation on `power logistic` is beyond the scope of this book, but I will present an example. Suppose we have been asked to calculate the sample size needed for a study. The Y variable being predicted is whether a person voted in the most recent school board election (1 if they voted; 0 if they did not). We want to estimate the effect of a college degree (1 if they have a BA or higher; 0 if they do not). Thus, a college degree is our binary X variable.

We decide to control for gender by adding it as a covariate (1 if the person is female, 0 if they are male). We will call this binary variable Z.

Assumptions. Power analysis is no better than the accuracy of our assumptions. Where do we get the values for our assumptions? Often, this is the hardest part. If we are lucky, we have a pilot study we can use. If not, we would need to search the literature and consult experts in the field. Here are the assumptions we will make in this particular power analysis. These assumptions are likely unrealistic, but we can use them to illustrate how to use `power logistic`:

1. Our goal is to estimate the effect of the X variable.
2. We want a power of 0.80.
3. We want an alpha of 0.05.
4. We assume that 35% of the population voted in the school board election. $\Pr(y = 1) = 0.35$, which we specify with the `py(0.35)` option.
5. We assume that 40% have a college degree. $\Pr(X = 1) = 0.40$, which we specify with the `px(0.40)` option.
6. We assume that 52% of the population is female. $\Pr(Z = 1) = 0.52$, which we specify with the `pz(0.52)` option.
7. We assume that 25% of men ($Z = 0$) who do not have a college degree ($X = 0$) voted. Conditional $\Pr(Y = 1|X = 0 \text{ and } Z = 0) = 0.25$, which we specify with the `pycondx0z0(0.25)` option.
8. We assume that 30% of women ($Z = 1$) who do not have a college degree ($X = 0$) voted. Conditional $\Pr(Y = 1|X = 0 \text{ and } Z = 1) = 0.30$, which we specify with the `pycondx0z1(0.30)` option.

Here is the `power logistic` command and the results:

```
. power logistic, power(0.80) alpha(0.05) py(0.35) px(0.40) pz(0.52) ///
> pycondx0z0(0.25) pycondx0z1(0.30)
Estimated sample size for logistic regression odds-ratio test
Likelihood-ratio test
H0: OR_X = 1  versus  Ha: OR_X != 1
Study parameters:
        alpha =    0.0500
        power =    0.8000
        delta =    2.2501  (odds ratio)
      oratiox =    2.2501
           px =    0.4000
           pz =    0.5200
           py =    0.3500
   pycondx0z1 =    0.3000
   pycondx0z0 =    0.2500
Estimated sample size:
            N =       218
```

The results indicate that we require an estimated sample size of $N = 218$, and the entered probabilities would correspond to OR of 2.250. There are different ways to select assumptions. For instance, instead of entering the probabilities for various combinations, we could input estimated logistic regression coefficients or ORs that we wish to detect.

15.3 Small-sample bias

It can be shown that a small sample-size N leads to a positive bias, making estimated ORs farther from 1.0 than they are in the population. This means that positive and negative effects may be slightly exaggerated using maximum likelihood estimates on a small sample. `lbw_working.dta` has just 189 cases, which is generally considered negligible. Thus, we may have overestimated or underestimated the true Bs and ORs. To avoid this problem, we can use a community-contributed command, `firthlogit` (Coveney 2008)[2] (see Heinze and Schemper [2002] and Firth [1993]), with a small sample.

2. You need to run `ssc install firthlogit` to download and install the command.

Firth logistic regression adds a penalty term to the likelihood function. It is appropriate when you have a small sample and a rare outcome and are concerned about perfect prediction. In our logistic regression, we have seven independent variables (`smoke`, `age`, `lwt`, `ht`, `ftv`, `2.race`, and `3.race`). With a very small sample predicting a very rare event, seven variables might perfectly predict the outcome, resulting in zero degrees of freedom. With a small sample and a relatively rare event, logistic regression may struggle to converge. Even if it does converge, it may produce extremely large coefficients. Firth's penalty helps convergence and reduces extreme size coefficients. Regularization terms stabilize the estimation and reduce overfitting (see Uno, Noma, and Gosho [2024]).

We run the logistic regression and store the results. Then we run the `firthlogit` command and store those results. Finally, we produce a table comparing the estimates:

```
. logistic low i.smoke age c.lwt i.ht c.ftv i.race
  (output omitted)
. estimates store logistic
. firthlogit low i.smoke age c.lwt i.ht c.ftv i.race
  (output omitted)
. estimates store firth
. estimates table logistic firth, b(%5.3f) se(%5.3f) p(%5.3f)
  (output omitted)
```

Here is the comparison of the logistic regression estimates of the Bs and their p-values with the same results using the Firth method. Notice that the parameter estimates for Firth logistic regression are smaller in absolute value for all but one of the coefficients. In this case, using the Firth method would keep all substantive and statistical conclusions about the model the same.

Independent variable	`logistic` B/p-value	`firthlogit` B/p-value
Smoke	1.073	1.031
	0.006	0.006
Age	−0.023	−0.022
	0.526	0.533
Weight at last menstruation	−0.017	−0.016
	0.011	0.016
Hypertension	1.748	1.626
	0.012	0.013
Visits during first trimester	0.037	0.045
	0.829	0.783
Black*	1.242	1.188
	0.018	0.019
Other*	0.930	0.897
	0.030	0.032
Intercept `_cons`	0.787	0.642
	0.497	0.566

*White is the reference group.
**Legend: B/Probability

15.4 Relative risk

The relative risk (RR) is another measure of effect size that is an alternative to the OR. The RR has a simpler interpretation in appropriate cases. Imagine that RR = 2.0 for people having a stroke in the next five years if they are morbidly obese compared with if they are not morbidly obese. What does this mean? Quite simply, morbidly obese people are twice as likely to have a stroke as people who are not morbidly obese. It is common to read popular news articles where the author misinterprets the ORs as the RR. This is a mistake because the OR overestimates the RR. For example, one of our early models found that smoking doubles the odds of having a low-birthweight newborn. This does not mean that smoking doubles the *risk* of a low-birthweight newborn. While the RR is easier to interpret correctly than an OR, it gives you only a relative measure, not the estimated actual risk. We get the estimated risk with the `margins` command; the RR is just the ratio of those estimated risks.

The RR and OR will be very similar if the outcome is a rare event under a 10% chance. In that case, misinterpreting the OR as an RR may not be egregious. An example would be an extensive national survey asking people if they had a stroke in the last 12 months. Studies involving large representative samples and relatively rare outcomes will have an RR $\cong$ OR. For studies that have less rare outcomes, the OR can substantially overestimate the RR (Ranganathan, Aggarwal, and Pramesh 2015). Unfortunately, the RR is not always appropriate.

What is the difference? Let us reexamine the relationship between the odds of having a low-birthweight newborn and whether the mother was a smoker.

```
. tabulate low smoke

           |   Smoked during
Birthweigh |     pregnancy
   t<2500g | Nonsmoker     Smoker |     Total
-----------+----------------------+----------
        No |        86         44 |       130 
       Yes |        29         30 |        59 
-----------+----------------------+----------
     Total |       115         74 |       189 
```

The odds of having a low-birthweight newborn are higher for smokers ($30/44 = 0.682$) than for nonsmokers ($29/86 = 0.337$), resulting in an OR of $0.682/0.337 = 2.024$. This means that the odds of a smoker having a low-birthweight newborn are about double the odds for a nonsmoker.

This seems simple enough, but it is important to appreciate that this is not the RR. The risk for smokers was $30/74 = 0.405$ or 40.5%. For nonsmokers, the risk was much lower, just $29/115 = 0.252$. The RR for smokers (chance for smokers divided by chance for nonsmokers) is $0.405/0.252 = 1.607$. Thus, the risk of a low-birthweight newborn for smokers is 1.607 times the risk for mothers who do not smoke.

$$\text{RR} = \frac{\frac{N(\text{low and smoke})}{N(\text{smoke})}}{\frac{N(\text{low and not smoke})}{N(\text{not smoke})}} = 1.607$$

We have already discussed how Stata's **logistic** command is a shortcut for the general linear model based on the binomial family of distributions and how the logit link function can predict the outcome. Running **logistic low i.smoke** is simply a convenient shortcut for actually running

```
. glm low i.smoke, family(binomial) link(logit) eform
```

The **eform** option specifies that we want the coefficients to be exponentiated as the ORs. To estimate RR, we use a different link function. Instead of using the logit link, we use the log link. Let us see how this relates to RR.

For comparison, we will run logistic regression to estimate the OR:

```
. logistic low i.smoke
Logistic regression                                     Number of obs =    189
                                                        LR chi2(1)    =   4.87
                                                        Prob > chi2   = 0.0274
Log likelihood = -114.9023                              Pseudo R2     = 0.0207

------------------------------------------------------------------------------
         low | Odds ratio   Std. err.      z    P>|z|     [95% conf. interval]
-------------+----------------------------------------------------------------
       smoke |
      Smoker |   2.021944   .6462989     2.20   0.028      1.08066    3.783112
       _cons |   .3372093   .0724103    -5.06   0.000     .2213694    .5136667
------------------------------------------------------------------------------
Note: _cons estimates baseline odds.
```

This shows that $\text{OR} = 2.02$, $z = 2.20$, and $p = 0.028$.

Then we run the **margins** command to get the expected risks for smokers and non-smokers:

```
. margins i.smoke
Adjusted predictions                                    Number of obs = 189
Model VCE: OIM
Expression: Pr(low), predict()

------------------------------------------------------------------------------
             |            Delta-method
             |     Margin   std. err.      z    P>|z|     [95% conf. interval]
-------------+----------------------------------------------------------------
       smoke |
   Nonsmoker |   .2521739    .040495     6.23   0.000     .1728052    .3315427
      Smoker |   .4054054   .0570741     7.10   0.000     .2935421    .5172687
------------------------------------------------------------------------------
```

The RR is the ratio, $0.405/0.252 = 1.607$.

If we wanted to get the RR of having a low-birthweight newborn for mothers who smoked, along with the p-values and confidence intervals, we would run the **glm** command using the log link:

```
. glm low i.smoke, family(binomial) link(log) eform
Iteration 0:  Log likelihood =  -158.1967
Iteration 1:  Log likelihood = -115.13416
Iteration 2:  Log likelihood = -114.90379
Iteration 3:  Log likelihood =  -114.9023
Iteration 4:  Log likelihood =  -114.9023
Generalized linear models                         Number of obs   =        189
Optimization     : ML                             Residual df     =        187
                                                  Scale parameter =          1
Deviance         =  229.8045995                   (1/df) Deviance =   1.228902
Pearson          =  188.9999998                   (1/df) Pearson  =   1.010695
Variance function: V(u) = u*(1-u)                 [Bernoulli]
Link function    : g(u) = ln(u)                   [Log]
                                                  AIC             =   1.237061
Log likelihood   = -114.9022998                   BIC             =  -750.4021

------------------------------------------------------------------------------
             |                 OIM
         low | Risk ratio   std. err.      z    P>|z|     [95% conf. interval]
-------------+----------------------------------------------------------------
       smoke |
      Smoker |   1.607642   .3433245     2.22   0.026     1.057812    2.443262
       _cons |   .2521739    .040495    -8.58   0.000     .1840819    .3454532
------------------------------------------------------------------------------
Note: _cons estimates baseline risk.
```

Notice that RR $= 1.608$, $p = 0.026$.[3] This applies to the ratio of the two risks and is another way of saying that the estimated probability of a low-birthweight newborn for smokers is greater than the estimated probability for nonsmokers. The RR (1.608) is substantially smaller than the OR (2.022). The gap would be even greater with an outcome where both possibilities were closer to equally likely. We could run the **margins** command in conjunction with RR and get the same estimated risks for smokers and nonsmokers as we got with the logistic regression command for the ORs.

A problem with estimating the RR is that maximum likelihood estimation may have difficulty converging with models with more than a few predictors. Stata may report that the iterations do not converge even after hundreds of them. By contrast, if we use **glm** with **link(logit)**, we usually get convergence after just a few iterations. For example, we can use the **glm** command for the logistic solution using

```
. glm low i.smoke age c.lwt i.ht c.ftv i.race, family(binomial) link(logit) eform
```

The solution converges after three iterations. When we use the **glm** command for estimating the RR using

```
. glm low i.smoke age c.lwt i.ht c.ftv i.race, family(binomial) link(log) eform
```

The solution fails to converge after 300 iterations.

3. The **glm** estimate of 1.608 is calculated with more precision than our hand-calculated RR of 1.607.

When is the RR inappropriate? In a case–control study, only the OR is meaningful. A case–control study samples retrospective information from a pool of people known to have the outcome. An example would be people who have had a heart attack in the last 12 months. This group is compared with a similar sample from a pool of people who do not have the outcome.

The RR that you get is very different if you have a case–control study than if you have a representative sample from the population. Therefore, you cannot generalize to the population based on your clinical trial. The OR gives the same result in a case–control study as in a study using a representative sample. This invariance for the OR lets you generalize to the general population using a case–control retrospective study. The lack of this invariance for the RR means that the RR for your case–control study is not meaningful for the general population. The OR is recommended over the RR when you have a case–control study.

This may be easiest to understand via an example using hypothetical data. Suppose that we are testing a widely used drug by people who are at least 70 years old. We want to assess the risk of a stroke within 12 months of starting the drug. We will need a large sample because having a stroke is rare in 12 months. Because this is a hypothetical study, we will think big and say we can get a sample of 100,000 adults.

Let us assume that just 5.1% (5,100) of the overall population of older people have a stroke in 12 months, and 94.9% (94,900) do not. We find that 29,600 of the 100,000 people in our sample use the drug. Check the marginal totals in the table below:

Side effect	Used drug	No drug	Total
Stroke victim	3,000	2,000	5,100
Nonstroke victim	26,600	68,400	94,900
Total	29,600	70,400	100,000

We discover the alarming fact that 3,000 (10.1%) of the 29,600 people who have used the drug have a stroke. We need to compare this with the risk for people who have not used the drug. We find that 2,000 of the 70,400 people who do not use the drug have a stroke. Thus, 2.8% of those not using the drug have a stroke compared with the much higher 10.1% of those who have had the drug.

Using the formula for the OR, we get

$$\text{OR} = \frac{3000}{26600} \Big/ \frac{2000}{68400} = 3.857$$

Using the formula for the RR, we get

$$\text{RR} = \frac{3000}{29600} \Big/ \frac{2000}{70400} = 3.568$$

Thus, with the representative sample of adults and a low incidence rate for the outcome, we find that the OR overestimates the RR.

We would have a hard time getting funding to collect these data on a representative sample of 100,000 adults, so we use a case–control (retrospective) study of 300 people who had a stroke and 300 people did not have a stroke.

Below are the results:

Side effect	Used drug	No drug	Total
Stroke victim	180	120	300
Nonstroke victim	84	216	300
Total	264	336	600

$$\text{OR} = \frac{180}{84}\Big/\frac{120}{216} = 3.857$$

$$\text{RR} = \frac{180}{264}\Big/\frac{120}{336} = 1.909$$

The bottom line is that you must use the OR instead of the RR in a case–control study. Whether you have a representative sample of the population or a case–control study, I strongly advise using the `margins` command to estimate the risks. You can find several YouTube videos that discuss when you need to use the odds ratio. In your internet browser, go to https://www.YouTube.com and search for "Relative Risk vs Odds Ratio! EXTENSIVE VIDEO". This is a detailed presentation of about 25 minutes. Your search will also list other (mostly shorter) videos comparing RR ratios with ORs.

A Appendix

Here is the do-file that reproduces the results in this book.

```
* logistic.do
* Alan C. Acock
clear
set scheme stsj // Makes graphs monochrome. Delete if you want color.

**# CHAPTER 1: WHAT WE CAN DO WITH LOGISTIC REGRESSION
* These commands produce figure 1.1 but are not shown or
* discussed in the chapter.
clear
webuse nhanes2l
logistic highbp bmi
margins, at(bmi=(16(2)50))
marginsplot, title("Estimated risk of high blood pressure by BMI")          ///
    ytitle("Probability of high blood pressure") xtitle("BMI")

**# CHAPTER 2: GETTING READY
clear
* 2.1 Opening the dataset
webuse lbw
* 2.2 Exploring the data
describe
summarize age lwt bwt smoke ht race low ftv
* 2.3 Labeling values for categorical variables
label define yesno 0 "No" 1 "Yes"
label values ht low yesno
describe age lwt bwt smoke ht race low ftv
ssc install fre, replace // Run this command to install fre.
fre low ht
fre race
* 2.4 Saving the edited dataset
save "lbw_working", replace
use "lbw_working", clear
```

```
**# CHAPTER 3: CONVENTIONAL OLS REGRESSION VERSUS LOGISTIC REGRESSION
* click File->Open recent, and open "lbw_working.dta"
clear
use "lbw_working"
* 3.1 What OLS regression can tell us
regress bwt i.smoke c.lwt i.ht, beta baselevels vsquish
margins i.smoke
lincom lwt*20
predict resid, residuals
histogram resid, freq normal
* 3.2 What logistic regression can tell us
glm low i.smoke c.lwt i.ht, family(binomial) link(logit) eform
logit low i.smoke c.lwt i.ht, vsquish baselevels
logistic low i.smoke c.lwt i.ht, vsquish baselevels
* Box 3.1
logit low i.smoke c.lwt i.ht, vsquish baselevels
logistic low i.smoke c.lwt i.ht, vsquish baselevels coef
logit low i.smoke c.lwt i.ht, vsquish baselevels or
logistic low i.smoke c.lwt i.ht, vsquish baselevels
* 3.2.1 Robust and cluster-robust estimation
logit low i.smoke
estimates store Base
logit low i.smoke, vce(robust)
estimates store Robust
estimates table Base Robust, se(%8.4f) p(%4.3f)
webuse hospid1, clear
fre hospid
logit low i.race i.smoke i.ht, baselevels
estimates store nocluster
logit low i.race i.smoke i.ht, baselevels vce(cluster hospid)
estimates store cluster
estimates table nocluster cluster, se(%8.4f) p(%4.3f)

**# CHAPTER 4: INTERPRETING AN ODDS RATIO
clear
* 4.1 What is an odds ratio?
use "lbw_working"
tabulate low smoke, column
logistic low i.smoke, baselevels vsquish
* 4.2 Interpreting ORs as a percentage difference for binary predictors
fre race
recode race (1 = 1 "White") (2 = 0 "Other") (3 = 0 "Other"), generate(white)
logistic low i.white, baselevels vsquish
```

```
**# CHAPTER 5: WHAT IS WRONG WITH OLS REGRESSION FOR A BINARY OUTCOME?
* This chapter requires you to enter the data by hand.
clear

* 5.1 Hypothetical data
input id divorced positives
1 0 8
2 0 10
3 0 7
4 0 7
5 0 8
6 0 4
7 0 10
8 0 9
9 0 7
10 1 5
11 1 1
12 1 4
13 1 2
14 1 3
15 1 4
16 1 7
17 1 3
18 1 4
19 1 0
20 1 1
end
list id divorced positives

* 5.2 How does logistic regression fit better than OLS linear regression?
* These commands produce figure 5.1 but are not shown or
* discussed in the chapter.
label variable divorced "Divorce status"
label variable positives "Positive comments"
scatter divorced positives, title("Raw data")
graph save raw.gph, replace
logistic divorced positives
predict div_predicted
scatter div_predicted positives, title("Logistic regression estimate")        ///
   ytitle("Estimated Pr(divorced)")
graph save log.gph, replace
regress divorced positives
predict div_pred, xb
scatter div_pred positives, title("Linear regression estimate")               ///
   ytitle("Estimated Pr(divorced)")
graph save ols.gph, replace
graph combine raw.gph ols.gph log.gph

**# CHAPTER 6 FITTING AND INTERPRETING LOGISTIC REGRESSION MODELS
clear

* 6.1 Interpreting coefficients and odds ratios
display exp(0.6932)
display ln(2.0001)

* 6.2 Fitting logistic regression models with multiple predictors
use "lbw_working"
logit low i.smoke c.age c.lwt i.ht c.ftv i.race,                              ///
    baselevels vsquish
logistic low i.smoke c.age c.lwt i.ht c.ftv i.race,                           ///
    baselevels vsquish
```

```
* 6.3 Interpreting ORs for quantitative predictors
display exp(-0.017*30.575)
display exp(-0.017*10)
lincom 30.57515*lwt, or
lincom 10*lwt, or

* 6.4 Selecting the right base level for categorical predictors
logistic low i.smoke c.age c.lwt i.ht c.ftv ib2.race,                ///
    baselevels vsquish

**# CHAPTER 7 HOW WELL DOES THE MODEL FIT THE DATA?
clear

* 7.1 Pseudo-R^2 measures of fit
use "lbw_working"
logistic low i.smoke c.age c.lwt i.ht c.ftv i.race, baselevels vsquish
* Run search spost13 to install the fitstat command.
fitstat
logistic low
logistic low i.smoke c.age c.lwt i.ht c.ftv i.race, baselevels vsquish
predict yhat if e(sample)
ttest yhat, by(low)

* 7.3 Identifying cases that the model fits poorly
logistic low i.smoke c.age c.lwt i.ht c.ftv i.race, baselevels vsquish
predict z, rstandard
list id z if z > 1.96 | z < -1.96

**# CHAPTER 8 SENSITIVITY AND SPECIFICITY
clear

* 8.2 Estimation of sensitivity and specificity
use "lbw_working"
logistic low i.smoke age c.lwt i.ht c.ftv i.race, baselevels vsquish
estat classification

**# CHAPTER 9 ROC CURVES AND CUTPOINTS FOR SCREENING TESTS
clear

* 9.1 ROC curves
use https://stats.idre.ucla.edu/stat/stata/notes/hsb2
fre prog
recode prog (1 = 0 "Not academic") (3 = 0 "Not academic")            ///
    (2 = 1 "Academic"), generate(academic)
fre academic
table math academic
roctab academic math, detail graph summary                            ///
    text(-.15 0 "Perfect specificity" -.15 .95 "Zero specificity")
ssc install cutpt, replace // Run this command to install cutpt.
cutpt academic math

* 9.2 Comparing tests
roccomp academic math science, graph summary
```

```
**# CHAPTER 10 PREDICTIONS USING THE MARGINS COMMAND
clear
* 10.2 Data preparation
webuse nhanes2l
summarize highbp age bmi sex
fre highbp sex
label define hi 0 "No" 1 "Yes"
label values highbp hi
recode sex (1=0 "Male") (2=1 "Female"), generate(female)
fre highbp female
save "nhanes2l_working", replace
* 10.3 Estimating the ORs
logistic highbp c.age c.bmi i.female, baselevels vsquish
* 10.4 The margins command
predict prob
* 10.4.1 Estimating risk for categorical predictors
table highbp female, statistic(percent, across (highbp))
logistic highbp c.age c.bmi i.female, baselevels vsquish
margins i.female
margins, dydx(i.female)
* 10.4.2 Estimating the risk for quantitative predictors
margins, at(age=(20(10)70))
* 10.4.3 Estimating for a combination of categorical and quantitative variables
margins i.female, at(c.age=(20(10)70))
margins i.female, at(age=(20 40 70) bmi=(20 30 50))
margins i.female, at(age=(32.5) bmi=(26))

**# CHAPTER 11 GRAPHIC PRESENTATION USING THE MARGINSPLOT COMMAND
clear
* 11.2 Graphs of categorical predictors that include three or more categories
use "nhanes2l_working"
recode hlthstat (5=1 "Poor") (4=2 "Fair") (3=3 "Good") (2=4 "Very good")      ///
   (1=5 "Excellent"), generate(hlthnew) label(cat5)
label variable hlthnew "Self-reported health"
save "nhanes2l_working", replace
logistic highbp age bmi i.female i.hlthnew, baselevels vsquish
testparm i.hlthnew
margins i.hlthnew
marginsplot
contrast rb3.hlthnew, effects or
logistic highbp age bmi i.female ib3.hlthnew, baselevels vsquish
* 11.3 Graphs with one quantitative predictor
margins, at(bmi=(15(5)60))
marginsplot, title("") ytitle("Pr(High blood pressure)")
* 11.4 Graphs with one quantitative and one categorical predictor
logistic highbp age bmi i.female i.hlthnew
margins i.female, at(bmi=(15(2.5)50))
marginsplot, title("") ytitle("Pr(High blood pressure)")
* 11.5 Graphs of a pair of categorical predictors
logistic highbp age bmi i.female i.hlthnew
margins i.hlthnew#i.female
marginsplot, title("") ytitle("Pr(High blood pressure)") xlabel(, angle(45))
```

```
* 11.6 Graphs with a pair of quantitative predictors
logistic highbp age bmi i.female i.hlthnew
margins, at(bmi=(15(5)50) age=(20 40 70))
marginsplot, title("") ytitle("Pr(High blood pressure)")                    ///
    plot1opts(msymbol(Oh) msize(large)) plot2opts(msymbol(Sh) msize(large))  ///
    plot3opts(msymbol(dh) msize(large))

**# CHAPTER 12 CURVE FITTING WITH QUADRATIC MODELS
clear

* 12.1 A hypothetical example of a quadratic model using OLS regression
input length score
10 50
30 60
50 70
70 80
90 85
110 86
120 80
140 60
160 30
180 20
200 15
end
label variable length "Individual session length (minutes)"
label variable score "Average score on final"
list length score
twoway (scatter score length)
twoway (lowess score length)
regress score length, beta
twoway (lfit score length) (scatter score length) (lowess score length)

* 12.2 Estimating the curve (uncentered predictor)
regress score c.length##c.length
margins, at(length=(10 30 50 70 90 110 120 140 160 180 200))
marginsplot, title("")

* 12.4 Estimating the curve (centered x)
* ssc install center, replace // Run this command to install center.
center length
summarize length c_length
regress score c.c_length##c.c_length, vsquish
margins, at(c_length=(-95 -76 -56 -36 -16 5 15 35 55 75 95))
marginsplot, title("")
```

```
* 12.6 Use of quadratic with logistic regression
use "nhanes2l_working", clear
* These commands produce figure 12.6 but are not shown or
* discussed in the chapter.
generate bpsystol_ln = ln(bpsystol)
twoway (lfit bpsystol_ln bmi),                                          ///
    ytitle("Estimated logit for high blood pressure")
logistic highbp c.bmi c.houssiz, vsquish
margins, at(bmi=(15(5)60))
marginsplot, title("") ytitle("Pr(High blood pressure)")
logistic highbp c.bmi##c.bmi c.houssiz, vsquish
margins, at(bmi=(15(5)60))
marginsplot, noci title("") ytitle("Pr(High blood pressure)")
center bmi
logistic highbp c.c_bmi##c.c_bmi c.houssiz, vsquish
margins, at(c_bmi = (-13(5)35))
marginsplot

**# CHAPTER 13 INTERACTION
clear
* 13.2 Interaction of a categorical and a quantitative variable using logistic
*      regression
use "nhanes2l_working"
logistic highbp i.female c.age c.houssiz
generate femaleXage = female * age
logistic highbp c.houssiz female c.age femaleXage
logistic highbp i.female##c.age c.houssiz, baselevels vsquish
* 13.3 Estimating and interpreting probabilities (uncentered)
margins i.female, at(age=(20(10)70))
marginsplot, title("") ytitle("Pr(High blood pressure)")
margins r.female, at(age=(20(10)70))
marginsplot, yline(0) title("")                                         ///
    ytitle("Difference in risk of high blood pressure")
margins, dydx(female) at(age=(20(10)70))
* 13.4 Interaction of categorical variables
logistic highbp i.female##i.hlthnew, baselevels vsquish
margins i.hlthnew#i.female
marginsplot, title("") ytitle("Pr(High blood pressure)") xlabel(, angle(45))
margins r.female@hlthnew
marginsplot, yline(0) title("")                                         ///
    ytitle("Difference in risk of high blood pressure") xlabel(, angle(45))
* 13.5 Interaction of quantitative variables
logistic highbp c.age c.bmi
margins, at(age=(20(15)65) bmi=(20 30 50))
marginsplot, noci title("") ytitle("Probability of high blood pressure")
logistic highbp c.age##c.bmi
margins, at(age=(20(15)65) bmi=(20 30 50))
marginsplot, title("") ytitle("Pr(High blood pressure)")                ///
    plot1opts(msymbol(Oh) msize(large)) plot2opts(msymbol(Sh) msize(large))   ///
    plot3opts(msymbol(dh) msize(large))
```

```
**# CHAPTER 14 RUNNING NESTREG AND POSTESTIMATION COMMANDS
clear
* 14.1 Nested logistic regression
use "lbw_working"
logistic low i.smoke
logistic low i.smoke i.race i.ht
logistic low i.smoke i.race i.ht c.ftv
nestreg, lrtable: logistic low (i.smoke) (i.ht i.race) (c.ftv), vsquish
* 14.2 Selected postestimation commands
logistic low i.smoke i.race i.ht, baselevels vsquish
contrast b2.race, effects or
test 1.smoke = 1.ht
use "nhanes2l_working", clear
fre region
logistic highbp i.region age race, baselevels vsquish
logistic highbp ib2.region age race, baselevels vsquish
quietly logistic highbp i.region age race, baselevels vsquish
testparm i.region
quietly logistic highbp ib2.region age race, baselevels vsquish
testparm ib2.region

*# CHAPTER 15 SPECIAL TOPICS
clear
* 15.1 Collinearity and multicollinearity
use "lbw_working"
generate agem = age*12
logistic low c.age c.agem, vsquish
* 15.1.1 Evaluating multicollinearity
quietly regress low i.smoke age c.lwt i.ht c.ftv i.race
estat vif
* 15.2 Sample size
power logistic, power(0.80) alpha(0.05) py(0.35) px(0.40) pz(0.52)          ///
    pycondx0z0(0.25) pycondx0z1(0.30)
* 15.3 Small-sample bias
logistic low i.smoke age c.lwt i.ht c.ftv i.race
estimates store logistic
ssc install firthlogit, replace // Run this command to install firthlogit.
firthlogit low i.smoke age c.lwt i.ht c.ftv i.race
estimates store firth
estimates table logistic firth, b(%5.3f) se(%5.3f) p(%5.3f)
* 15.4 Relative risk
tabulate low smoke
logistic low i.smoke
margins i.smoke
glm low i.smoke, family(binomial) link(log) eform
```

References

Acock, A. C., and M. L. DeFleur. 1972. A configurational approach to contingent consistency in the attitude-behavior relationship. *American Sociological Review* 37: 714–726. https://doi.org/10.2307/2093582.

Allison, P. D. 2012a. *Logistic Regression Using SAS: Theory and Application*. 2nd ed. Cary, NC: SAS Institute.

———. 2012b. When can you safely ignore multicollinearity? Statistical Horizons, https://statisticalhorizons.com/multicollinearity/.

———. 2013. What's the best *R*-squared for logistic regression? Statistical Horizons, https://statisticalhorizons.com/r2logistic/.

Clayton, P. 2013. cutpt: Stata module for empirical estimation of cutpoint for a diagnostic test. Statistical Software Components S457719, Department of Economics, Boston College. https://ideas.repec.org/c/boc/bocode/s457719.html.

Coveney, J. 2008. firthlogit: Stata module to calculate bias reduction in logistic regression. Statistical Software Components S456948, Department of Economics, Boston College. https://ideas.repec.org/c/boc/bocode/s456948.html.

Cox, D. R., and E. J. Snell. 1989. *Analysis of Binary Data*. Vol. 32 of *Monographs on Statistics and Applied Probability*, 2nd ed. London: Chapman and Hall/CRC.

Cragg, J. G., and R. S. Uhler. 1970. The demand for automobiles. *Canadian Journal of Econometrics* 3: 386–406. https://doi.org/10.2307/133656.

Firth, D. 1993. Bias reduction of maximum likelihood estimates. *Biometrika* 80: 27–38. https://doi.org/10.1093/biomet/80.1.27.

Heinze, G., and M. Schemper. 2002. A solution to the problem of separation in logistic regression. *Statistics in Medicine* 21: 2409–2419. https://doi.org/10.1002/sim.1047.

Hosmer, D. W., Jr., S. Lemeshow, and R. X. Sturdivant. 2013. *Applied Logistic Regression*. 3rd ed. Hoboken, NJ: Wiley. https://doi.org/10.1002/9781118548387.

Iacobucci, D., M. J. Schneider, D. L. Popovich, and G. A. Bakamitsos. 2016. Mean centering helps alleviate "micro" but not "macro" multicollinearity. *Behavior Research Methods* 48: 1308–1317. https://doi.org/10.3758/s13428-015-0624-x.

Jann, B. 2004. center: Stata module to center (or standardize) variables. Statistical Software Components S444102, Department of Economics, Boston College. https://ideas.repec.org/c/boc/bocode/s444102.html.

———. 2007. fre: Stata module to display one-way frequency table. Statistical Software Components S456835, Department of Economics, Boston College. https://ideas.repec.org/c/boc/bocode/s456835.html.

Jegerlehner, S., F. Suter-Riniker, P. Jent, P. Bittel, and M. Nagler. 2001. Diagnostic accuracy of a SARS-CoV-2 rapid antigen test in real-life clinical settings. *International Journal of Infectious Diseases* 109: 118–122. https://doi.org/10.1016/j.ijid.2021.07.010.

Lazarsfeld, P. F. 1958. Evidence of inference in social research. *Daedalus* 87: 99–130.

Long, J. S., and J. Freese. 2014. *Regression Models for Categorical Dependent Variables Using Stata*. 3rd ed. College Station, TX: Stata Press.

McDowell, A., A. Engel, J. T. Massey, and K. Maurer. 1981. "Plan and operation of the Second National Health and Nutrition Examination Survey, 1976–1980". In *Vital and Health Statistics*. Hyattsville, MD: National Center for Health Statistics. https://stacks.cdc.gov/view/cdc/13005/cdc_13005_DS1.pdf.

McFadden, D. 1974. "Conditional logit analysis of qualitative choice behavior". In *Frontiers in Econometrics*, edited by P. Zarembka, 105–142. New York: Academic Press.

———. 1987. Regression-based specification tests for the multinomial logit model. *Journal of Econometrics* 34: 63–82. https://doi.org/10.1016/0304-4076(87)90067-4.

Mitchell, M. N. 2020. *Data Management Using Stata: A Practical Handbook*. 2nd ed. College Station, TX: Stata Press.

Nagelkerke, N. J. D. 1991. A note on a general definition of the coefficient of determination. *Biometrika* 78: 691–692. https://doi.org/10.1093/biomet/78.3.691.

O'Brien, R. M. 2007. A caution regarding rules of thumb for variance inflation factors. *Quality and Quantity* 41: 673–690. https://doi.org/10.1007/s11135-006-9018-6.

Ranganathan, P., R. Aggarwal, and C. S. Pramesh. 2015. Common pitfalls in statistical analysis: Odds versus risk. *Perspectives in Clinical Research* 6: 222–224. https://doi.org/10.4103/2229-3485.167092.

Tjur, T. 2009. Coefficients of determination in logistic regression models–a new proposal: The coefficient of discrimination. *American Statistician* 63: 366–372. https://doi.org/10.1198/tast.2009.08210.

Uberti, L. J. 2022. Interpreting logit models. *Stata Journal* 22: 60–76. https://doi.org/10.1177/1536867X221083855.

Uno, S., H. Noma, and M. Gosho. 2024. Firth-type penalized methods of the modified poisson and least-squares regression analyses for binary outcomes. *Biometrical Journal* 66: e202400004. https://doi.org/10.1002/bimj.202400004.

Wasserstein, R. L., and N. A. Lazar. 2016. The ASA statement on *p*-values: Context, process, and purpose. *American Statistician* 70: 129–133. https://doi.org/10.1080/00031305.2016.1154108.

Williams, R. 2012. Using the margins command to estimate and interpret adjusted predictions and marginal effects. *Stata Journal* 12: 308–331. https://doi.org/10.1177/1536867X1201200209.

Wölfl-Duchek, M., F. Bergmann, A. Jorda, M. Weber, M. Müller, T. Seitz, A. Zoufaly, R. Strassl, M. Zeitlinger, H. Herkner, H. Schnidar, K. Anderle, and U. Derhaschnig. 2022. Sensitivity and specificity of SARS-CoV-2 rapid antigen detection tests using oral, anterior nasal, and nasopharyngeal swabs: A diagnostic accuracy study. *Microbiology Spectrum* 10: e02029–21. https://doi.org/10.1128/spectrum.02029-21.

Wooldridge, J. M. 2010. *Econometric Analysis of Cross Section and Panel Data*. 2nd ed. Cambridge, MA: MIT Press.

Author index

A

Acock, A. C. 115
Aggarwal, R. 154
Allison, P. D. 50, 102, 147, 148
Anderle, K. 56

B

Bakamitsos, G. A. 102
Bergmann, F. 56
Bittel, P. 56

C

Clayton, P. 65
Coveney, J. 151
Cox, D. R. 49
Cragg, J. G. 50

D

DeFleur, M. L. 115
Derhaschnig, U. 56

E

Engel, A. 70

F

Firth, D. 151
Freese, J. 47, 51, 52, 98, 149

G

Gosho, M. 152

H

Heinze, G. 151
Herkner, H. 56
Hosmer, D. W., Jr. 7

I

Iacobucci, D. 102

J

Jann, B. 11, 103
Jegerlehner, S. 56
Jent, P. 56
Jorda, A. 56

L

Lazar, N. A. xv
Lazarsfeld, P. F. 115
Lemeshow, S. 7
Long, J. S. 47, 51, 52, 98, 149

M

Massey, J. T. 70
Maurer, K. 70
McDowell, A. 70
McFadden, D. 49
Mitchell, M. N. 10
Müller, M. 56

N

Nagelkerke, N. J. D. 50
Nagler, M. 56
Noma, H. 152

O

O’Brien, R. M. 147

P

Popovich, D. L. 102
Pramesh, C. S. 154

R

Ranganathan, P. 154

S
Schemper, M. 151
Schneider, M. J. 102
Schnidar, H. 56
Seitz, T. 56
Snell, E. J. 49
Strassl, R. 56
Sturdivant, R. X. 7
Suter-Riniker, F. 56

T
Tjur, T. 50

U
Uberti, L. J. 78
Uhler, R. S. 50
Uno, S. 152

W
Wasserstein, R. L. xv
Weber, M. 56
Williams, R. 78, 121
Wölfl-Duchek, M. 56
Wooldridge, J. M. 15

Z
Zeitlinger, M. 56
Zoufaly, A. 56

Subject index

A

additive model 109, 131–132

B

base level 44–46, 141–143
binary variables 10

C

categorical and quantitative variables 75–78
categorical predictors 72–74
center community-contributed command 103
centering the predictor 102
cluster sampling 26–28
collinearity 145–146
    essential 102
    nonessential 102
contrast command 83, 139
correlate command 146
COVID-19 55–56
Cox–Snell R^2 49–50
cutpoint 65–66
cutpt community-contributed command 65

D

describe command 8
diminishing gap 121

E

edit dataset 13–14
end of a command 42
estat vif postestimation command 146–148
estimates store command 25–26
estimates table command 25–26
estimating the curve 103–105

F

false negatives 55
false positives 56
Firth logistic regression 152–153
firthlogit community-contributed command 151–153
fitstat community-contributed command 48–50
fre community-contributed command . . . 11–12, 27, 31, 61, 70, 135

G

Graph Editor 85–86

H

hierarchical modeling 134
hypothetical data 35–36

I

imperfect model 25–26
import from SAS 4
import from SPSS 4
information criteria 52
    Akaike 52
    Bayesian 52
interaction 115–132
    categorical variables 117–119, 124–127
    quantitative variables 117–119, 127–132
intercept-only model 49
interpreting coefficients 39–40

interpreting odds ratios 39–40
intersectionality 115

L

labeling values 10–12
linear model 38
linked variables 98
Liu method 65
`logistic` command 22
logistic regression 20–24
`logit` command 22
`lowess` command 95
lowess curve 95–97

M

`margins` command 69–78
  `dydx()` option 74, 123
`marginsplot` command 79–91
McFadden's R^2 49–50
model fits poorly 53
multicollinearity 145–148
multiple predictors 41–42

N

nearest to $(0,1)$ method 65
nested logistic regression 134–138
`nestreg` command 133–143

O

odds ratios 29–31, 71
one quantitative and one categorical predictor 89
one quantitative predictor 86–88
ordinary least-squares regression 15–20

P

pair of categorical predictors 90
pair of quantitative predictors 91
percentage difference 31–33
`power logistic` command 149–151
`predict` command 50–51, 72
pseudo-R^2 measures of fit 47–51

Q

quadratic models 93–114
quadratic with logistic regression 106–114
quantitative predictors 42–44, 74–75

R

receiver operating curves 60–66
`recode` command 31, 80
reference group 44–46
`regress` command 15–20
  `baselevels` option 16
  `beta` option 16
relative risk 153–158
reporting results 2–4
robust and cluster estimation 24
`roccomp` command 66–67
`roctab` command 62–65
  `detail` option 62
  `graph` option 62
  `summary` option 62
  `text` option 64

S

sample size 148–151
save dataset 13–14
scatterplot 95
session length 101
small-sample bias 151–153
`spost13` community-contributed package 47

T

`tabulate` command 29
`test` postestimation command 139
`testparm` postestimation command 143
Tjur's D 51
true negative 55–56
true positive 55–56
`twoway` command 95
  `scatter` subcommand 95

U

uncentered
model . . . 102
predictor . . . 97–102
quantitative variables . . . 116
results . . . 119

V

variance inflation factor . . . 147
variance–covariance matrix . . . 27

W

working directory . . . 14

Y

Youden method . . . 65

Z

z score . . . 53
zone of transition . . . 37